School Choice

Peter W. Cookson, Jr. School

Yale University Press

Choice   The Struggle for the Soul
of American Education

New Haven and London

For Carla

Set in Bodoni types by Marathon Typography Service,
Durham, North Carolina.
Printed in the United States of America by Vail-Ballou Press,
Binghamton, New York.

Library of Congress Cataloging-in-Publication Data
Cookson, Peter W.
    School choice : the struggle for the soul of American education /
[Peter W. Cookson, Jr.].
        p.   cm.
    Includes bibliographical references (p.) and index.
    ISBN 0-300-05791-1 (cloth)
            0-300-06499-3 (pbk.)
    1. School choice—United States.   I. Title.
LB1027.9.C67   1994
371'.01—dc20   93-35450
                                                            CIP

A catalogue record for this book is available from the British
Library.

The paper in this book meets the guidelines for permanence and
durability of the Committee on Production Guidelines for Book
Longevity of the Council on Library Resources.

10 9 8 7 6 5 4 3 2

Contents

Prologue   A Journey of a Thousand Opinions

School choice has captured the imagination of American educators, policymakers, and the public. Most of what is written about school choice, however, has been highly partisan, even ideological. The purpose of this book is to place the school choice movement in its historical and contemporary contexts, to describe the major choice plans through case studies, to analyze the outcomes of school choice, and to examine the underlying assumptions of the market model of educational reform. At the end of the book I suggest how public education can be "reinvented," using school choice as one innovative mechanism. At a more fundamental level, this book is also about the social and educational dilemmas facing Americans today. Any book on educational reform cannot help but reflect on America's love affair with the idea of education and the sobering educational, political, and social realities of a nation that finds itself economically threatened and socially fragmented. No book about education today can ignore the plight of American children or the struggles of families and educators who must cope with inadequate resources and antiquated knowledge at a time when science has brought us to the very edge of a great intellectual transformation. Nor can a book about school choice be mute about the profound philosophical, moral, and political issues concerning individual rights, collective responsibilities, and the struggle for a good society. The drama over school choice represents a moral struggle of genuine significance. At the risk of sounding overly dramatic, we might say that the very soul of American education is at stake.

Roughly five years ago, I had the opportunity to hear a well-known social theorist speak about school choice and its benefits. He also played a tape recording made by Seymour Fliegel, the former deputy superintendent of schools in East Harlem, New York, who spoke passionately about what choice had done to improve education for the poor children of Community School District 4. I was fascinated by the topic and by the extravagant claims made for school choice, which struck several sociological nerves; after all, the reform literature asserts that there is only a weak relationship between school governance and student achievement. Was school choice a miracle cure for American education? At that time I did not know that District 4 had received more financial support than most other school districts in New York City. I had not visited Central Park East Secondary School in District 4 and learned about Deborah Meier, the charismatic principal. I had not yet learned that before there was choice in District 4 there were alternative schools, and that Anthony Alvarado, superintendent of schools in District 4 in the early 1970s, had likened school choice to rearranging the deck chairs on the Titanic (Harrington and Cookson 1992). Five years ago I was unaware that the Manhattan Institute, a conservative think tank on the Upper East Side of Manhattan, had taken a deep interest in District 4. And finally, I had not had an opportunity to read the data published under the aegis of the institute which claimed that choice is related to higher reading scores, and to conclude that these data were unreliable and unconvincing.

In short, I have learned that to understand the politics of school choice, one must understand the politics of educational reform and personal reputation. And one must understand how deeply the educational system has become enmeshed in the continuing struggle between those who believe in a society based on traditional community values and those who believe that individual self-interest promotes collective well-being. In one of my last interviews for this book I asked an eminent school reformer whom I should speak to next about school choice. He thought for a second or two and then answered, "Chris Whittle." Christopher Whittle is an entrepreneur who has introduced commercialized television into American classrooms and is the founder of the Edison Project. The purpose of the Edison Project is to establish a thousand private schools throughout the country that will compete with public schools. I asked myself, Can it be that Christopher Whittle is the John Dewey of the twenty-first century? Traditionally, many Americans have believed that cognition best serves commerce, but should commerce shape and control cognition?

In the past five years I have immersed myself in the school choice controversy. I have written articles, engaged in debates, and tried to read the vast literature that has grown up around this reform. I have traveled from California to Minnesota to Massachusetts, visiting schools, parent information centers, and state boards of education. I interviewed the director of the Center for Choice in Education in the U.S. Department of Education and visited the White House when former President Bush announced the "G.I. Bill Opportunity Scholarships for Children." Every state in the Union has been surveyed concerning school choice legislation. I have engaged in what amounts to a running conversation with hundreds of people about school choice. It is indeed a journey of at least a thousand opinions. These people included policymakers, politicians, teachers, academics, parents, students, and school administrators. I have listed many of these generous people in the acknowledgments. Some of them will not agree with the conclusions I draw about school choice, but I have tried to listen to their views as empathetically as possible. In research it is important not only to hear what people say, but to understand how they reason. The surface remark may not be as instructive as the assumptions that lie behind it. Thus, this study can be read at two levels. At the level of school policy, I describe the varieties of school choice and the data available concerning the relationship between school choice and student, school, and social outcomes. At the sociological level, my interest is in the cultural context of the school choice movement and its relationship to the rapidly changing American society.

I have been working in schools and universities for more than twenty years, as a teacher in public and private schools and as an administrator at the elementary school and university levels, and I am a sociologist of education. I have witnessed educational reforms emerge, flower, and seemingly disappear, only to return years later under new rubrics. In the late 1960s, as a caseworker for the New York City Department of Social Services, I had the opportunity to watch the battle over school decentralization on the ground. I saw communities ripped apart through racial antagonism and observed the fear that can grip a community in turmoil. But I also saw hope. I learned that poor people are as deeply committed to their children's education as more privileged parents are. I have tried to ground myself in the politics of education through experience, observation, and participation. And I have spent more than fifteen years studying private and public schools, as well as school effectiveness and international educational reform.

To understand the significance of the school choice movement in American education and life, the social scientist must be a kind of geologist. The future of American education will be determined not by the winds that glide over the educational landscape but by the hidden seismic faults that push against each other and threaten to cause an educational earthquake. To understand this reform, one must accept the dialectic tension between its practical applications and the moral theater it generates. To describe school choice merely in terms of governance is like describing a painting as pigment on canvas.

I do not think school choice alone can resolve our educational crises. We need a strong public school system if our country is to survive. We also need, however, to recognize that without change the public school system is liable to collapse from its own bureaucratic weight. School choice can create communities of parents, students, and educators and encourage families and students to exercise the educational freedom essential for a vibrant democracy. As we shall see, school choice plans differ dramatically. One cannot be for or against school choice in general, one can only respond to specific plans. Some school choice plans are silly and even dangerous, others are sensible and safe. But even the safest and most sensible plan can never be more than a tactic of reform; a genuine strategy of educational reform requires a more profound, more lasting, and more structural commitment to families, teachers, and children than even the most sophisticated student enrollment policy. School choice without good schools is meaningless.

In writing this book I have shared ideas with an extraordinary group of thinkers. I was particularly fortunate at the very beginning of my research to interview Charles V. Willie of the Harvard Graduate School of Education; Professor Willie has written about school choice and has implemented school choice plans in several American cities. Toward the end of my research I talked to him about what I had learned. His observations brought into focus a fundamental principle of educational reform: School reform policies that are not driven by a sense of educational and social justice are bound to fail. Excellence and equity are not meaningful alternatives, because without equity there can be no excellence. It is this principle, which so much writing about educational reform misses, that has helped me to understand the limits and possibilities of school choice.

The organization of this book is straightforward. Chapter 1 examines the cultural context from which the school choice movement arose. Chapter 2 outlines the historical development of school choice in its social and philosophical contexts. Who is for school choice and why? To what degree do advocates of school choice adequately describe the American public school system? Chapter 3 explores school choice in action. I describe the legislative picture and present case studies of choice plans in the state of Minnesota; in Cambridge and Fall River,

Massachusetts; in East Harlem and White Plains, New York; and in Milwaukee. In what ways does choice matter? Can we identify tangible outcomes of choice? Chapter 4 assesses what we know about the outcomes of school choice in terms of student achievement, school improvement, equity, and community. Chapter 5 reflects on and analyzes market models of educational reform and the competitive metaphor that underlies them. Chapter 6 extends what has been learned about school choice through this research and argues for a democratic vision of educational reform.

Acknowledgments

The study of school choice has provided me with an opportunity to be part of a complex, extended, and sometimes heated conversation about how American education can be improved. Without the generosity, enthusiasm, and intelligence of many individuals, this book could not have been written. I am deeply indebted to them.

In particular, I would like to thank the following people for sharing with me their expertise about the politics and practices of school choice: Mike Alves, Tom Andert, Stephen Arons, David Baker, Pat Bauch, Clint Bolick, Kathy Borman, Frank Brown, Bill Burrow, Bea Carson, Sophia Catsambis, John Chubb, James Coleman, Joe Conaty, Jack Coons, Bruce Cooper, Bob Crain, Debra Cruel, Kevin Dougherty, Frank Echols, Don Erickson, Seymour Fliegel, Frances Fowler, Michelle Fine, Margaret Gallagher, Nathan Glazer, Charles Glenn, Ellen Goldring, Ivor Goodson, Maureen Hallinan, Linda Darling-Hammond, Diane Harrington, R. Fred Hess, Harold Himmelfarb, David Hogan, Fred Houle, Pat Howlett, Peggy Hunter, Mike Johanek, Karen Karp, Jack Klenk, Sally Kilgore, Ted Kolderie, David Labaree, Ellen Lagemann, Valerie Lee, Henry

Levin, Ann Lieberman, Myron Lieberman, Pat Lines, John Maddaus, Roslyn Mickelson, Joe Nathan, Perry Price, Mary Anne Raywid, Bella Rosenberg, Kathryn Schiller, Mark Schmidt, Daryl Sedio, Albert Shanker, Rina Shapira, Ted Sizer, David Stevenson, Stephen Sugarman, Jeremy Sykes, Geoffrey Walford, Jim Wallace, Amy Stuart Wells, Doug Willms, John Witte, Julia Wrigley, Saul Yanofsky, and Laurette Young.

Three people have been critically important in guiding my thinking about school choice. Caroline Hodges Persell has been my colleague for many years and has shared with me her observations about the limits and possibilities of markets to reform education; the work of Barbara Schneider has brought to the choice controversy empirical rigor and analytic insight. She has enabled me to untangle the complexity of who chooses schools and to what effect; Charles V. Willie helped me to create a framework for understanding the choice movement and the possibilities inherent in choice for reforming American education.

I have been motivated to write this book because I am concerned about the future of American children. Jonathan Kozol has written passionately about the consequences of societal indifference to poor children. Deborah MacFarlane has dedicated her life to improving the educational and life chances of America's poorest adults and children. From each I have drawn inspiration.

My colleagues at Adelphi University have been extremely supportive. I would like to thank Mary Botta, Ann DiPietro, Martha Meyer, and Arline Cavanaugh of the School of Education. Diane Caracciolo's willingness to take on extra responsibilities in the School of Education made it possible for me to pursue my scholarship. Kristina Berger provided valuable research assistance, humor, and analytic insight throughout the writing of the book. The faculty of the School of Education have shared with me their views about school choice. I have benefited a great deal from their contributions. I would like to thank, in particular, Alan Sadovnik and Susan Semel for their insights and constructive irreverence. The administration of Adelphi has made it possible for me to conduct my research and write the book. I would like to thank Vice Provost Harvey Wiener, Provost Igor Webb, and President Peter Diamandopoulos for their encouragement and practical support. The dean of the School of Education, Jeffrey Kane, has been my friend and colleague for several years; our discussions about school choice have been extremely illuminating. His intellectual honesty and love of the human spirit have opened my eyes to the possibilities of a genuine humanistic education.

Philip Altbach and Edith Hoshino provided me with an opportunity to edit a special issue of *Educational Policy,* and in doing so helped me to educate myself about the complexities of the topic. Gracia Alkema encouraged me to edit *The Choice Controversy,* which also provided me with more learning opportunities.

Gladys Topkis, senior editor at Yale University Press, had faith in this project from its inception and has helped me to sharpen my thinking about school choice. Our friendship is invaluable to me. Harry Haskell's copyediting improved the text immeasurably.

I am fortunate to have a loving family. My children, Alexandra and Aram, help to keep things in perspective with humor and good sense. My wife Susan's dedication to social justice and creative integrity has motivated me for over twenty-five years. Without her encouragement and love, I would not have been able to write this book.

On July 21, 1993, my colleague and friend Carla A. Hernandez died; she was twenty-four. She was a lover of life and a true educator. Her ideas and beliefs weave through this book like a seamless web.

1 Lifestyle Loyalties in an Age of Doubt

Ten years ago school choice was little more than a twinkle in the eyes of a handful of civil libertarians. Concerned by what they saw as a monopoly state system of education, they argued that American public schools were robbing citizens of their right to choose their children's education. It was a matter of conscience and constitutionality. The eloquence of their arguments notwithstanding, the ethos of the common school was so deeply embedded in American folklore and consciousness that for most citizens personal liberty and collective effort did not seem to be in conflict. Public schools were supposed to create a common culture; besides, private schools offered an alternative to the public system. On balance, the governance of public education seemed to function fairly well; most Americans felt that whatever was wrong with schools could be attributed to inadequate teachers and undemanding curriculum. By the late 1980s, however, school choice had become the hottest educational reform idea on the policy horizon. The debate over

1

school governance continues today. The school choice movement has become a crusade for those who believe that without educational liberty there can be no educational justice or innovation.

In this chapter we examine the cultural context from which the school choice movement arose. Why school choice now? What particular elements of American society and culture give credibility to the belief that competition is more likely than cooperation to improve schools? Are the underlying assumptions concerning the operations of markets in congruence or conflict with the assumptions underlying democracy? Clearly, these are fundamental questions, and we should not be surprised that the controversy over school choice has aroused public passions. The national debate not only has a political and educational context but also a deep philosophical and moral subtext. The context is about school improvement, but the subtext is about values, identity, and freedom. Undoubtedly, school choice has become infused with emotion because it is an educational reform that goes directly to the heart of an American dilemma. What is the correct balance between individual and family freedom and the rights of the community? All of us have strong feelings about how to resolve this dilemma. Thus, it is not surprising that school choice has become a kind of reform Rorschach test into which people read their own feelings about the relationship between school and society.

Rustbowl Schools/Rainbow Dreams

Since the 1980s Americans have experienced what amounts to a national panic attack about the condition of their children and their schools. Squeezed by inadequate resources and waves of poor immigrant children, public school systems in virtually every large American city are collapsing: dropout rates hover well above 50 percent, truancy is the norm rather than the exception, violence is common, students struggle for basic literacy, often without success, a great deal of teaching is uninspired, and the physical condition of the schools is a disgrace. Most inner-city schools have the look of crumbling fortresses; broken windows are left unrepaired and the paint is peeling in so many places that the schools would appear aban-

doned if it were not for the children. The playgrounds are cracked and lit-
tered asphalt patches. These are the "savage inequalities" about which
Jonathan Kozol (1991) writes so eloquently and so poignantly. The children who attend these schools very often experience hardships that make a
mockery of ordinary conceptions of childhood.

The condition of American children is so profoundly serious that at a
very basic level it could be said that all American children are at risk. To
cite but a few examples: one-fourth of all preschool-age children in the
United States live in poverty; each year roughly 350,000 children are born
to mothers who were addicted to cocaine during pregnancy; 15 million children are being reared by single mothers whose incomes average a little over
eleven thousand dollars a year; on any given night approximately 200,000
American children have no home; each year child protection agencies
receive over two million reports of child abuse and neglect (Hodgkinson
1991:10). In a *Time* magazine article called "Shameful Bequests to the Next
Generation," Nancy Gibbs (1990:42) observed: "Every eight seconds of the
school day, a child drops out. Every 26 seconds, a child runs away from
home. Every 47 seconds, a child is abused or neglected. Every 67 seconds,
a teenager has a baby. Every seven minutes, a child is arrested for a drug
offense. Every 36 minutes, a child is killed or injured by a gun. Every day
135,000 children bring their guns to school." Clearly, education is operating
in a cultural milieu that is hostile and even violent toward children.

American education is also in an intellectual crisis. In a culture that
glorifies materialism, there is little room for the development of children's
critical capacities. What should we teach our children to prepare them to
live in the next century? Our curricula are outdated, our pedagogy is anti-
quarian, our method of preparing teachers preposterous. It is difficult to
grow intellectually when the content of learning is of no apparent use-
value. This is all the more paradoxical because we are living in an age of
enormous scientific, technological, and intellectual breakthroughs. Children are not learning enough and they are not learning the right things.
The materialism of contemporary culture has called the very purpose of
education into question—do we educate citizens or create consumers? We
are living in a society in which spiritual and moral purpose seems like a

vestige of a bygone era. At some deep level we must ask ourselves why we expect children and young people to spend so much time in institutions that can be bad for their mental and even physical health. We must wonder why so many educators seem more interested in the politics of pedagogy and curricula than in nurturing children to become intellectually capable and ethically strong adults.

To compound this educational malaise, from the 1960s on public education became increasingly politicized and culturally fragmented. Civil rights leaders have been divided as to whether public schools should be mechanisms for integrating different cultures and races, or whether they should serve particular communities that may or may not wish to associate with different races or ethnic groups. Which is more important, ethnic integration or ethnic pride? Racial conflict has created a virtual state of educational apartheid, drawing public schools into the ongoing controversy over racial integration. Moreover, the banishment of prayer from the public schools offended many religious Americans and outraged Protestant fundamentalists. To make matters worse in the eyes of fundamentalists, many of the public educators who banished prayer endorsed sex education. Some religious families began to withdraw their children from the public schools and started their own private schools. Public schools became lightning rods for public dissatisfaction with a society that seemed to have forgotten the basics. Public schools were repositories of "relativism" and incubators of incompetence. The dream of a vibrant public school system that could mitigate the divisive effects of race and class and educate young people for productive lives became tarnished in the public mind. Public schools were not the "great equalizers" hoped for by their founders; the common-school ethos held little meaning for an increasing number of Americans.

The School Choice Crusade

The fragility of the public school system has provided a window of opportunity for those reformers who believe that there can be no educational transformation without changing the very structure of American public education. In the 1980s, these reformers were carried into the mainstream of educational policy-making by a rising tide of conservatism that swept up from the Southwest, where free enterprise and antigovernment sentiments dominated public discourse. It became fashionable to ridicule "social engineering" and soft-hearted liberals. There was a loss of faith in public institutions, which were often pictured by conservatives as being expensive, self-interested, and incompetent. Some conservative critics argued that liberal social welfare policies actually created more inequality rather than less. The basic democratic metaphor seemed to lack resonance with many people. This lack of confidence in democracy was indicated by how few people chose to vote in local, state, and national elections from the early 1970s to the early 1990s.

The loss of faith in public institutions and democracy paved the way for a new secular faith that drew its inspiration not from the democratic social metaphor of community and cooperation, but from the market social metaphor of individual interest and competition. In the 1980s the market metaphor gained new credibility and moved from the wings of the social theater to take center stage. The dominant policy voices of the 1980s sang the song of marketplace miracles. They implied that by a kind of social magic private vices, such as greed, become public virtues because greed energizes the few to create material surpluses that eventually trickle down to the many. Whereas previously the social Darwinistic assumptions underlying the market metaphor had been muted in public consciousness, in the 1980s markets were elevated to social and economic icons. Because of the ascendancy of the market faith, by the early 1990s privatizing public education became a credible policy in the eyes of certain reformers, newspaper reporters, and educational policymakers.

Contemporary school choice advocates, who invariably believe in the social and educational efficacy of market competition, argue that public education must be redesigned from the ground up if we are to create schools that are humane and intellectually productive and that can prepare children for the next century. As I have discovered, most choice advocates are educational revolutionaries. They have little use for traditional reforms, little tolerance for compromise, and little patience for what they perceive to be the mediocrity and self-interest of the public school establishment. In

1991, for instance, Dr. Stephen Guffanti, a forty-year-old physician from Vista, California, gave up his lucrative medical practice to join the school choice crusade. As the leader of Parents for Educational Choice, Dr. Guffanti spearheaded a campaign to place on the California ballot a proposal that would require the state to provide an annual $2,500 voucher for every school-age child wanting to transfer from public to private school. Stephen Guffanti's faith in educational competition is suffused with a sense of mission: "To me, it's so perfectly clear that we have a monopoly school system, a one-size-fits-all school system that doesn't fit anybody." Like Don Quixote, Dr. Guffanti is driven by an impossible dream; tilting at policy windmills can motivate true believers even when their enemies are illusory, or perhaps because their enemies are illusory. Forty million young people go to school every day—without a strong public school system, many of these young people would have no schools at all. Moreover, Dr. Guffanti is wrong—American public education is far from being a one-size-fits-all school system.

The school choice movement is a loose confederation of individuals and groups with little in common except a deep contempt for public education as we now know it. Civil libertarians, evangelicals, alternative public school advocates, free marketers, civil rights advocates, some Catholic educators, and maverick school superintendents share a desire to undo the current system of public education and create schools that are answerable to consumers. In a world where consumption and choice are considered essential for the good life, the idea that children are required to attend a particular public school in their neighborhood seems anachronistic, even reactionary. The political orientations of these revolutionaries are mixed. There is a school choice movement from the left which generally favors public school choice, and there is a school choice movement from the right which generally favors publicly funded vouchers for private schools.

There can be little doubt that without the coming to power of Ronald Reagan, school choice as an educational reform would never have reached national prominence. The Reagan revolution challenged the public school system at a very basic level. As the leader of a powerful conservative movement, Reagan legitimated a political philosophy that was essentially antigovernment and probusiness. The Reagan revolution waged ideological war against government spending, wasteful public institutions, and the welfare state in general. George Bush carried forward Reagan's social agenda and expanded on Reagan's notions of educational reform, particularly when he proposed the "G.I. Bill Opportunity Scholarships for Children" in June 1992. The President introduced the bill with great fanfare at the White House. The audience that witnessed the signing was composed primarily of inner-city African-American parents, evangelical ministers, Republican politicians, and school choice grass-roots organizers. Prior to the announcement, the President met with school choice advocates from around the nation, including Rev. Pat Robertson, Sen. Strom Thurmond of South Carolina, and multimillionaire conservative Pierre Du Pont. Each of these men represents an important element of the school choice movement of the right: religion, the politics of race, and markets.

The President defended school vouchers by arguing that the "G.I. Bill for Children" was similar to the G.I. Bill for Veterans in that the money families would receive from the government would not flow directly to the schools themselves. The President said, "For too long, we've shielded schools from competition—allowed our schools a damaging monopoly power over our children. And this monopoly turns students into statistics and turns parents into pawns. And it is time we begin thinking of a system of public education in which many providers offer a marketplace of opportunities—opportunities that give all of our children choices and access to the best education in the world" (Bush 1992). Equating school choice with a revolution in education, the President finished his presentation by saying, "And look at it this way, we're doing the Lord's work for our nation's future."

Whether or not school choice is the Lord's work, public opinion polls generally show that Americans support the idea. When, for instance, a poll conducted by *Phi Delta Kappan* (Elam 1990) asked parents whether or not they favored or opposed allowing students and their parents to choose among public schools regardless of where they live, roughly 62 percent of all respondents were in favor; 81 percent of non–public school parents were in favor. The poll found that men and women held similar views about school choice, but that nonwhites were more in favor of school choice than whites.

We know, however, that public opinion is highly volatile and that the results of polls can often be attributed to how questions are asked. It can be difficult to distinguish between the orchestrated media blitz that some school choice advocates have created and the feelings of the "average" American about this topic. A recent study by the Carnegie Foundation for the Advancement of Teaching (1992), for instance, calls into question how much the American people are in favor of school choice. In a survey of parents of children attending public school, 70 percent answered no to the following question: "Is there some other school to which you would like to send your child?" The choice these respondents were offered could be a public or a private school, within or outside the respondent's district. Moreover, 62 percent of the parents surveyed in the Carnegie study were against the issuance of private school vouchers funded at the public expense. And, surprisingly, 87 percent of these parents were either very satisfied or somewhat satisfied with the quality of the education their children received in 1991. These findings suggest that there is still strong support for the neighborhood school among American parents. Yet, my research tells me that the school choice movement is far more than an artifact of questionnaire design or media campaign. School choice is a grass-roots movement similar to other social movements such as gun control, abortion rights, and school prayer. School choice activists are similar to other social activists; they believe themselves to be morally empowered and are not likely to compromise with their opponents.

Choice, Culture, and Commodification

Scholars have differed as to why school choice has become the dominant reform idea of the current era. The sociologist Kevin Dougherty and the educator Lizabeth Sostre have attempted to explain the rise of the school choice movement through the "state-relative-autonomy" theory of political power and the "garbage-can theory of organizational decision-making" (Dougherty and Sostre 1992:160). The former theory hypothesizes that the state is a neutral arbiter, weighing and directing interest-group pressure; the latter theory, first proposed by James March and his associates over thirty years ago, makes the commonsensical point that people choose policies for conflicting reasons and because policies are available. Organizational leaders have short-term objectives and do not actually know what the consequences of their decisions will be. My experience in studying school choice, however, is that this reform symbolizes something intrinsic to American society. The ideals of individualism, autonomy, and competition run deep in the American character. I believe that we are in the midst of a profound cultural transition; the core consensus that united public opinion since the Great Depression has all but evaporated. An essential element of this consensus is the firm belief that public schools are the mediators of merit and the cradles of democracy. With the weakening of the consensus, however, traditional methods of educational reform appear inadequate and seemingly serve the self-interests of the public school establishment.

Educational reforms arrive on the political and educational scene because of complex social conditions and because certain social actors are able to place their perspective on the policy agenda for serious consideration (Popkewitz 1988, 1991). The sociologist Margaret S. Archer (1979:3) has written: "To understand the nature of education at any time we need to know not only who won the struggle for control but also how: not merely who lost, but how badly they lost." She reminds us that educational reform is not a laboratory science—it is created in the caldron of public beliefs, incomplete information, and class politics. Following the sociologist Emile Durkheim's observation that society precedes school, we can see that major educational reforms pass in and out of public favor depending on social conditions and how prevailing ideologies interpret these conditions. Karl Marx's argument that the ruling ideas in any era are generally the ideas of the ruling class may overstate the case, but the fundamental observation still rings true: ideas spring from and are embedded within the class structure, which, in turn, is shaped by the dominant economic method of production. There is a close linkage between what is thought to be an adequate education and changes in the economy. Is it any wonder that in a highly mobile, service-oriented economy, the neighborhood school would lose its luster and even many of its constituents?

During the 1980s the United States underwent a political, intellectual, economic, and cultural revolution of great magnitude. The social consensus forged by Franklin D. Roosevelt during the New Deal had run its course and came to a dramatic end on the killing fields of Southeast Asia and with the collapse of the Great Society. Opponents of the New Deal labeled social engineering expensive and ineffective. The economic foundation of the country shifted from east to west, from agriculture and industry to new technologies and multinational corporations. The cultural revolution of the 1960s had anticipated, if not created, a different kind of society. Somehow, "do your own thing" became transmuted into a social belief that acquisition and ambition were the moral prerequisites of the good life. Consumption and personal fulfillment replaced the older values of family, savings, and personal denial. The traditional middle-class values lost their cultural resonance and the media celebrated the cult of personality. Christopher Lasch (1979) wrote about the "culture of narcissism," where self-realization and self-fulfillment became a kind of collective obsession. The very definition of community shifted from its traditional anchors of family, neighborhood, church, lodge, and school to race, gender, occupation, and sexual preference. The media became intoxicated with novelty, and the America painted on the television screen every night is to a Norman Rockwell painting as a bikini is to overalls.

This new culture of self-fulfillment and acquisition was partially made possible by the withdrawal of the middle and upper middle class from public spaces and public commitments. During the 1970s class enclaves developed, especially in the suburbs, that are essentially self-contained and cut off from the larger community. Condominiums and suburban shopping malls may have communal areas, but few people use these "commons" for political debate or philosophical speculation. Moreover, these public spaces are often segregated by race and class. The popularity of class enclaves has created a culture where the art of consumption and personal interest can be highly developed. Shopping has become probably our most common and impassioned form of collective behavior. The idea that it is morally appropriate to segregate oneself from the larger society has become virtually unquestioned by those who have distanced themselves from the social problems of the inner city.

In sum, traditional loyalties have been replaced by what might be called lifestyle loyalties. These loyalties are based not on group affiliations but on individual preferences. Choosing is a critical element in developing a lifestyle. Advertising, which habitually confuses marketing with true choice, tells us that the good life consists of smart consumership. We are what we own. There seems little doubt that lifestyle loyalties represent a commodification of life that is probably unprecedented. In a bittersweet *New Republic* article entitled "The Tyranny of Choice," Steven Waldman, a Washington correspondent for *Newsweek*, writes (1992:23–25): "The topic of how much freedom brings has fascinated philosophers throughout the ages. But when Sartre urged man to embrace and acknowledge his own power to choose, he did not have in mind figuring out the difference between hair conditioner, rejuvenator, reconstructor and clarifier." Waldman points out that a typical supermarket in 1976 had nine hundred products; in 1992 it had more than thirty thousand. A cosmetic center outside Washington, D.C., carries about fifteen hundred types and sizes of hair care products. Twice as many cosmetic surgery operations are performed now as in the 1970s. In the 1980s a new religious denomination was formed every week. Examples could go on and on, but Waldman's point is clear. In fact, he makes several observations about choice: "Choice erodes commitment, choice takes too much time, choice awakens us to our failings, choice leads to inept consumption, choice causes political alienation, choice erodes the self, choice reduces social bonding."

Behind Waldman's sometimes satirical observations is some very good sociology. Lifestyle loyalties that are built around marketing and making empty choices can lead to serious confusion about the nature of identity and purpose. The superficiality about becoming loyal to a set of products rather than a group of people increases the likelihood of detachment and alienation from society. The culture of acquisition has permeated virtually all aspects of American society, but underneath this culture lie a set of structural changes that are not only redefining people's values and preferences but restructuring the society itself.

It is not by chance that the school choice movement arose at a time when many Americans felt a pervasive sense of doubt about the future direction of their society. The historian Paul Kennedy (1989) points out that the shift from "materials-intensive" to "knowledge-intensive" types of manufacturing has seriously undercut the economic foundation upon which the American dream historically has been built. Relative to many other industrialized countries, the United States is in a state of decline. Most Americans experience this by witnessing the flood of foreign products in their stores and on their roads. The Japanese, in particular, have threatened American economic hegemony. Some authors claim that the economic successes of the Japanese are attributable to their educational system (White 1987). In any case, America has become a debtor nation, owned, in good part, by foreign investors and suffering from chronically high unemployment. In the international industrial assembly line, the United States is increasingly on the receiving end rather than the giving end.

As the Japanese were threatening the United States economically, the more liberal immigration policies instituted in the 1960s allowed a great number of new immigrants to come to the United States. By the time a child born in 1992 is sixty-five, more than half of the individuals residing in the United States will trace their ancestry to Africa, the Hispanic world, the Pacific islands, North Africa, or Asia. By 1995 whites will be a minority in the public schools in at least ten states. The Los Angeles public school system already teaches children who speak eighty-one languages other than English at home. The historian Arthur Schlesinger, Jr., has written about the dis-uniting of America. His fear is that this ethnic and racial diversity will create an environment in which a sense of unity becomes impossible. Racism runs deep in American society; not only are racial and ethnic groups separated from each other by de facto segregation, but minorities are more likely to be unemployed than whites, have lower incomes than whites, and have higher mortality rates than whites. The infant mortality rate is higher in Harlem, New York, than in Bangladesh.

At the same time that America is becoming more multicultural, it is also becoming more polarized by wealth and income. We are reaching a point when we can speak of a divided society in which rich and poor are separated by grand canyons of inequality. The top 20 percent of American families earn 47 percent of all income and own at least three-quarters of all wealth, while the bottom 20 percent earn only 3.6 percent of all income and own virtually nothing. In 1986 the wealthiest 1 percent retained 15 percent of the total national income (Persell and Cookson 1992:47) and got

60 percent of the gain in the 1980s "boom" (Nasar 1992:A1). At the same time the number of people living in poverty in the United States skyrocketed. In 1983, 36 million people lived below the poverty line, an increase of 38 percent in six years. The political analyst Kevin Phillips maintains (1990:xix) that the distribution of wealth depended on "who controlled the federal government, for what policies, and in behalf of what constituencies." Phillips, who can hardly be accused of being a liberal, refers to the 1980s as the Second Gilded Age.

While the upper and upper middle classes were reaping the benefits of Reaganomics, the after-tax median income of American families actually declined in the 1980s (Phillips 1990). America's young families were particularly hard hit. According to the Children's Defense Fund, the median income of families with young children plunged by nearly one-third between 1973 and 1990. These income losses affected virtually every family with young children: white, African-American, Hispanic, married couples, and single parents (Johnson, Sum, and Weill 1992:2–3). Only those families headed by a college graduate experienced a slight increase in their median income between 1973 and 1990. At the same time that the United States was undergoing a profound cultural and economic transformation, the exchange value of educational credentials deflated considerably. A high school degree could no longer guarantee employment, and a college degree was no longer an automatic ticket to the good life. The power of education to lift the disadvantaged out of poverty into the mainstream almost evaporated. Education lost its luster, and even its intrinsic value was open to question. Many Americans were caught in the credential crunch, whereby their degrees and diplomas had little to do with their social mobility. When education loses its social power, it is vulnerable to attack.

In sum, the social, economic, and educational context from which the school choice movement arose was unlike any other period in American history. A patina of wealth masked serious economic problems. The rootlessness of much American life became transformed into lifestyles based on consumption and status, and social commitment to public institutions, with the exception of the military, virtually disappeared. The middle and upper middle class led increasingly "privatized" lives and millions of Americans fell into poverty. The condition of children became a national scandal. Public education was apparently failing to fulfill its historic mission of creating a literate, numerate, and socially conscious citizenry. It was under these circumstances that the school choice movement emerged from the margins of American education.

The Scope of School Choice

The phrase "school choice" covers a multitude of student assignment plans that vary significantly in their underlying assumptions and operational procedures. Their common denominator is that they encourage or require students and their families to become actively engaged in choosing schools. Whereas previously most American families simply sent their children to their neighborhood schools, the implementation of choice plans makes it possible for students to attend schools inside or outside their district, and sometimes even outside their city or town. As we will see, these plans have direct effects on student assignment policies and indirect effects on the design of American education.

Although the variety of school choice plans makes summarization difficult, a few major types can be identified. It is important to get a sense of these types early in the discussion because the voices raised in the choice controversy are not known for precision of expression. In this book the word *choice* refers to any student assignment policy that permits parents and children to participate in selecting a school. Some choice plans partially restrict the educational choices families can make, while others have virtually no restrictions. The former type of plan is often referred to as "controlled-choice" and the latter as "open-enrollment." Most choice plans fall near the middle of the continuum between the two types. Virtually every state in the Union has either enacted or is considering a choice plan that is uniquely configured by its political environment and educational problems. In chapter 3 we will examine in depth several major types of plans. Below are some basic "choice" definitions:

> *Intradistrict-choice.* A plan that allows students to choose schools within one public school district. Depending on the specific plan, the range of choice may include a few to all schools in a district.

Interdistrict-choice. A plan in which students may cross district lines to attend school. Tuition funds from the state follow the student, and transportation costs are usually provided. Unlimited interdistrict choice is equivalent to statewide open enrollment.

Intrasectional-choice. A plan that is limited to public schools.

Intersectional-choice. A plan that includes both public and private schools.

Controlled-choice. A student assignment plan that requires families to choose a school within a community, but choices can be restricted to ensure the racial, gender, and socioeconomic balance of each school. Often, such plans reflect a strategy to comply with court-ordered desegregation.

Magnet schools. Public schools that offer specialized programs, often deliberately designed and located so as to attract students to otherwise unpopular areas or schools. Magnet schools are often created to promote racial balance.

Postsecondary options. Programs that enable high school students to enroll in college courses at government expense. The courses they take may contribute to high school graduation requirements as well as to their college programs.

Second-chance programs. Alternative schools and programs for students who have difficulties in standard public school settings. Most often these students have either dropped out of school, are pregnant or are parents, have been assessed as chemically dependent, or have been expelled from their previous school.

Charter schools. Publicly sponsored autonomous schools that are substantially free of direct administrative control by the government but are held accountable for achieving certain levels of student performance (and other specified outcomes).

Workplace training. Apprenticeship programs to teach students a skilled trade not offered through present vocational training. Costs are divided between the employer and the school district.

Voucher plans. Any system of certificate or cash payments by the government that enables public school students to attend schools of their choice, public or private. Vouchers have a fixed value and are redeemed at the time of enrollment.

Tuition tax credits. A system of funding choice that allows parents to receive credit against their income tax if their child attends a nonpublic school. Such a system is, by definition, intersectional.

As we can see from the above definitions, tailoring a choice plan is itself a creative endeavor. Choice can be limited to one district and thus have minimal educational design consequences, or it can be statewide and intersectional and thus completely alter the way schools are organized within a state. Nobody has yet proposed an *inter*state choice plan and, as far as I know, nobody has seriously suggested a classroom choice plan. Thus, choice plans tend to fit within the traditional structure of American education. However, if the movement toward privatization of education accelerates, there may be new types of schools that do not fit within the traditional structure of American education. If, for example, the Edison Project is successful in franchising a thousand private schools, American education will be profoundly transformed. Moreover, if the New American Schools Development Corporation, which President Bush established in his "America 2000" educational plan, is able to create enough "break-the-mold schools" by using the resources of corporations, think tanks, community organizations, and vendors of educational products, then the mode by which educational services are delivered will be transformed. For now, however, most choice plans have been developed and implemented within the traditional parameters established by state constitutions and by traditional conceptions of a public school district.

2 Reformers and Revolutionaries
The Drama of Deregulation

To understand the school choice movement requires a grasp of its political roots and a sensitivity to its philosophical origins; the choice controversy touches on issues that go to the very core of American life. The drama over school choice and public school deregulation has created a public theater where personalities have clashed and ideas have come into conflict. In this chapter, we examine the elements of this drama and create a context by which to place historically, philosophically, and politically the beliefs and passions that characterize the school choice movement.

Thunder on the Educational Right

By the time Ronald Reagan was elected President in 1980, school reform was in the air. Reagan's political agenda for education, however, was unfocused. In general, he supported conservative causes and argued strongly for such policy initiatives as tuition tax credits and private school vouchers. In his campaign, Reagan had suggested that the Department of Education be abolished, charging that it was little more than another example of big-government Democrats' eagerness for spending public monies to make government even bigger. Still, abolishing any department of the federal government is difficult at best. Vested interests become institutionalized, and once institutions take hold in a political environment, they are extremely hard to dislodge or disband. All in all, therefore, the conduct of American education during the first two years of the Reagan presidency was pretty much business as usual—and the Department of Education survived.

In 1983, however, the National Commission on Excellence in Education, a blue-ribbon panel of educational leaders inside and outside of government, dropped a bombshell by way of its now-famous report *A Nation at Risk*. The picture the commission drew of American education was starkly pessimistic, even ominous: "Our Nation is at risk. Our once unchallenged preeminence in commerce, industry, science and technological innovation is being overtaken by competitors throughout the world. . . . The educational foundations of our society are presently being eroded by a rising tide of mediocrity that threatens our very future as a Nation and a people. . . . We must dedicate ourselves to the reform of our educational system for the benefit of all" (1983:1).

The report resonated with a general sense that, despite Reagan's cheerleading, something was wrong. The future was unclear; new challenges were threatening American smugness as number one. Significantly, the report began, "Our Nation is at risk," not "Our children are at risk." If we were failing, it was in good part because our schools were inadequate. Traditionally, Americans place a great deal of faith in education as a way of saving society from itself. Saviors, however, can easily become scapegoats in times of anxiety and doubt. In any case, the battle cry raised by the commission was echoed by other groups, including the Education Commission of the United States (1983), the Business Higher Education Forum (1983), the Carnegie Foundation for the Advancement of Teaching (1983), the Twentieth Century Fund (1983), the College Board (1983), and the National Governors Association (1986). A number of nationally recognized scholars, such as Mortimer Adler (1982), John Goodlad (1984), and Theodore Sizer (1984), also declared American public education a wasteland and provided a host of suggestions about how to make schools better.

In effect, the country in the 1980s and early 1990s engaged in what was possibly the greatest educational debate in its history. This debate can be divided roughly into three periods: 1983 to 1986, 1986 to 1989, and 1989 to the present. The first reform wave stressed the accountability of teachers and students. Forty-five states, for instance, raised their high-school graduation requirements. There was a greater emphasis on the evaluation of teachers and some states, like Arkansas, instituted competency tests for teachers (Hess 1992:7). The idea that simply raising standards would lead to greater student learning was, from a learning theory point of view, superficial at best. High jumpers do not break records simply because the level of the bar they are to jump over is raised. It is not surprising, therefore, that despite the attempts to legislate learning, standardized test scores continued to decline. Accountability alone could not transform schools.

The second wave of reform began in 1986, when the Carnegie Forum on Education and the Economy published *A Nation Prepared: Teachers for the Twenty-first Century*. The report called for restructuring schools through the professionalization of teaching and the empowerment of parents and students. Professionalization of teaching was institutionalized in school-based management innovations in such places as Dade County, Florida, and Rochester, New York. Parent and student empowerment resulted in two forms of policy options: radical decentralization and school choice. The most dramatic example of radical decentralization occurred in Chicago. The Chicago Reform Act, signed into law in December 1988, contained a number of elements, but by far its most dramatic component shifted centralized decision making to school-based management through local school councils at each of the city's 542 public schools. Each council is composed of six parents, two community representatives, two teachers, and the principal, elected by their own constituents (Hess 1992:13).

By the end of the decade, however, many educational reformers had come to believe that simply changing the internal organization of schools would not result in greater student learning because the very structure of the schools prohibited learning. What was needed was a transformation of the school systems themselves. The public school monopoly prohibited innovation because it was in the interest of professional educators to maintain the status quo. At this point some educators and policymakers began to suggest that in order to transform American schools, the so-called state monopoly of education would have to be broken. Thus, the reforms of the 1980s could be characterized as a movement from traditional notions of educational reform (such as improved teaching practices) to more radical notions (revamping the entire system). The conditions were ripe for a school choice coalition to emerge and challenge the educational establishment. The success of the new right in reshaping the American political, economic, and educational agenda made the idea of large-scale school choice credible. The philosophical foundations of choice, however, preceded the 1980s by over two hundred years. The concept of consumer sovereignty is embedded in American beliefs about what makes a good and just society.

The Origins of Choice
John E. Coons, law professor at the University of California at Berkeley, believes that school choice is the sword that will cut the Gordian knot of educational mediocrity. Coons has been a critic of the public school system for several decades. His reasons are moral and legal: for him, school choice is a matter of simple justice. "Our system of tax-supported education has for 150 years provided one of the primary embarrassments to America's image as a just society" (Coons 1992:15). Coons was one of the first proponents of a voucher system and has always been concerned with the ethical ends of school choice as well as with the means. In *Scholarships for Children* (1992), he and his colleague Stephen D. Sugarman essentially argue that school choice initiatives must include voucher components that favor the poor. For Coons, choice is an instrument of distributive justice and a medium of expression for the ordinary family; it serves the psychological welfare of the family; and it is the guarantor of a marketplace of ideas. In sum, school choice is synonymous with liberty. For him, the present system disregards family values because the child, in effect, is removed from the family's intellectual and moral beliefs by the government when he or she is

placed in a public school. Coons believes that choice is a way of overcoming the divisions between family and state.

Coons, Sugarman, and the constitutional lawyer Stephen Arons have been at the forefront of the part of the educational reform movement that seeks to disestablish the public school system in the name of freedom. They are the latest embodiment of a fundamental belief in individual freedom that goes back to the time of the seventeenth-century social philosopher John Locke. Civil libertarians such as Arons maintain that compulsory education violates individual conscience and the First Amendment to the Constitution. When we force children to attend state-run schools, we are creating a tyranny of mind that hides behind the mask of supposed cultural neutrality. While private schools allow for some freedom, their costs prohibit those who are not wealthy from escaping the public school system. The core belief of libertarians is that every individual is responsible for his or her behavior and that the state has no business controlling the minds of its citizens, young or old. Over one hundred years ago, John Stuart Mill wrote about state-sponsored education as follows: "It is a mere contrivance for molding people to be exactly like one another; and as the mold in which it cast them is that which pleases the predominant power in government, whether this be a monarch, a priesthood, an aristocracy, or the majority of the existing generation, in proportion as it is efficient and successful, it establishes a despotism over the mind" (quoted in Arons 1983:195).

Similar convictions had been aired from the time of the American Revolution. Thomas Paine advocated a voucher system, and the struggle to create a public school system throughout the nineteenth century aroused deep political passions (Ravitch 1974). Arons, whose book *Compelling Belief* documents how public schools can threaten individual conscience, expresses this belief as follows: "The freedoms or powers guaranteed by the First Amendment would be meaningless if government had within its legal power to dictate the desires, values, aspirations, world view, or ethics of individuals seeking to exercise these freedoms or powers. The specifics of the Amendment in any period must, therefore, be interpreted as a right to individual consciousness" (1983:96).

The educational philosopher Jeffrey Kane (1992:50) has echoed Arons's sentiments: "Who is to determine what individual children will know, how they should view the world, how they shall govern their actions with others and understand themselves? Who has the right, through the schools, to guide the emerging intellect and spirit of individual children?" In effect, civil libertarians argue that a sacred core within each human being is debased when the child is forced to attend a school that he or she might not wish to attend. There is a purity and a moral absolutism to these arguments that are appealing. They are, however, slightly misleading because the U.S. Supreme Court in this century has consistently upheld the right of families to send their children to nonpublic schools. The landmark case concerning the autonomy of private schools was *Pierce v. The Society of Sisters* in 1925, which dealt with the issue of whether children in Oregon could be compelled to attend public schools. The state legislature had passed an essentially anti-Catholic bill that was supported by the Ku Klux Klan. When the U.S. Supreme Court heard the case, it found that "[t]he child is not a mere creature of the State." According to Arons (1983:40), the "Court saw that schooling concerned socialization and development of the individual mind, and refused to make this influence the sole possession of the political majority."

Since the *Pierce* decision, public policy toward private schools has centered on two issues: regulation and funding. Because the American educational system is decentralized, each state has slightly different regulations concerning the operation of private schools, but almost all adopt a hands-off policy. Moreover, private schools do receive public dollars to maintain their programs (Cookson 1991a). Another important Supreme Court decision that supports student and parental rights in terms of freedom of choice is *Wisconsin v. Yoder* (1971). Writing for the majority in that case, Chief Justice Warren Berger amplified the right of educational choice. "[The public] high schools tend to emphasize intellectual and scientific accomplishment, self-distinction, competitiveness, worldly success, and social life with other students. Amish society emphasizes informal learning through doing, a life of 'goodness' rather than a life of intellect, wisdom rather than technical knowledge, community welfare rather than competition, and separation from rather than integration with contemporary worldly society" (quoted in Kane 1992:49–50).

Clearly, in principle and to some extent in reality, Americans already have a great deal of educational choice. The problem is that the tuition of private schools, especially good private schools, prohibits those who are not affluent from exercising this right. Thus, it has been argued that unless we provide all families with the financial resources required to attend private schools, certain families are not treated equally under the law, and this violates both our sense of social ethics and the Fourteenth Amendment to the Constitution. Civil libertarians argue that public education engages in monopolistic practices through compulsory education laws. Interestingly, both the right and the left have labeled the public educational system monopolistic, but for different reasons. To oversimplify slightly, the left tends to see public schools as controlled by the capitalist class. The socialist political economists Samuel Bowles and Herbert Gintis (1976) have argued that public education is little more than a mechanism for reproducing the class structure. Critics from the right accuse the public school system of being a bastion of fuzzy-thinking liberalism, secular humanism, and just plain mediocrity. One wonders, however, if American public education is in fact, as centralized, rationalized, and manipulative as its critics claim. To put the school choice controversy in perspective, it is extremely helpful to ground the discussion in the reality of how American public and private schools are governed and organized.

The Contours of American Education

One of the ironies of the 1980s was that the federal government became deeply involved in educational reform while at the same time arguing against federal involvement in social policy. This is doubly ironic because, in a legal sense, the federal government has very little authority over the public school system; it is the states that are responsible for public education. Moreover, the day-to-day administration of public schools is left to local authorities. Nonetheless, choice advocates inevitably argue that the public school system has historically precluded the right of choice (Everhart 1982). A former governor of Minnesota, Rudy Perpich (1989:A17), has described the public school system as "autonomous and answerable to virtually no one. Large, hidebound bureaucracies administer school districts of many cities, and often are too removed from the reality of the schoolroom to address the basic problems."

Playing off the title of the historian David Tyack's book *The One Best System* (1974), critics of the public school system have argued that monopolistic practices have destroyed school-based autonomy. Is this true? Between 10 and 11 percent of American elementary and secondary students attend private schools, most of them religious in nature. Public education does not, in a strict sense, monopolize the educational marketplace, although obviously public schools do *dominate* the marketplace. Even within the public sector, however, there is more diversity than the critics of public schools acknowledge. The political scientist John Witte suggests we think of state control as falling on a continuum from "decentralized diversity to monopolistic uniformity" (1990:13). A decentralized and diverse system, he writes, would consist of schools ranging widely in terms of size, age groupings, pedagogy, curriculum, teacher-student interaction, and social affiliations. Schools would be run by local authorities and private groups, and regulations would be held to a minimum. At the other end of the spectrum would be a national system of schools that are standardized in terms of size, grade structure, curriculum, teaching methods, and evaluation. Student achievement and advancement would be uniformly judged, most likely through nationally administered examinations. The central government would be the locus of authority and schools would be financed by national funds. Curiously, in their zeal for criticizing the American system, many school choice advocates hold European and Japanese schools up as models to emulate, although these systems are virtual educational monopolies. Many European states have state-controlled curricula and a national testing policy that ruthlessly sorts and selects students regardless of what type of school they attend.

If we were to place American schools on the continuum suggested by Witte, we would see that the American system is far closer to the decentralized-diversity end of the spectrum than it is to the monopolistic-uniformity end. There are over fifteen thousand public school districts in the United States, comprised of approximately sixty thousand elementary schools and over twenty-three thousand secondary schools (Witte 1990:15). Some public school districts are extremely large, but most have fewer than six hundred students. It is true that in certain urban public school systems, such as New York's, there has been a tendency toward bureaucratic control. The city of New York educates approximately nine hundred thousand students a year, has more cafeterias than Howard Johnson has restaurants, and has a budget of over four billion dollars. New York, however, is not representative of the rest of the United States. Most school systems are much, much smaller and much more integrated into their communities. Research has shown me that, contrary to the image created by public school critics such as Chubb and Moe (1990), most public school administrators are extremely responsive to parents and to the electorate on whom they depend for funds.

Witte also goes on to point out that the "one best system" in fact is highly diverse in terms of the grade organization of schools. For example, 45.6 percent of American secondary schools are organized from grades nine through twelve. This means that the majority of secondary schools are *not* organized in this manner. Moreover, if we examine schools in terms of their student-body composition, we see that there is tremendous variation according to geographic region. For instance, schools in some states, such as Maine, Vermont, New Hampshire, and Iowa, are almost completely white, while in other states, such as New Mexico, Mississippi, and Hawaii, white children are a minority, and student bodies in several large states, such as California and Texas, are extremely mixed racially. Inner-city schools have student populations that are nearly exclusively African-American, Hispanic, and Asian. Suburban schools tend to have few minorities, and rural schools fewer still. Schools also vary by the social-class composition of their student bodies, which directly reflects the socio-economic composition of their catchment areas.

In terms of curriculum and pedagogy, there are no monopolistic practices in the United States. As Powell, Farrar, and Cohen (1985) point out in *The Shopping Mall High School*, American education is a cacophony of curricula and teaching styles. In most American public schools, teachers have some latitude in determining how and sometimes what they will teach. I have worked in schools where teachers are encouraged to initiate new curricula and expected to adapt their pedagogical style to the needs of the students. It is true that not all public school teachers are highly motivated or imaginative, but the same could be said about private school teachers. In fact, from my research I would have to conclude that, by and large, pedagogical styles in private schools tend to be less imaginative and more "chalk-and-talk" than in public schools.

Furthermore, the authority structure in the American public school system is far from monopolistic. The federal government has no constitutional authority except in the area of enforcing civil rights. State departments of education are notoriously ineffective in ensuring that their regulations are enforced. Superintendents of school districts have little to do with what goes on within the classrooms in their districts, and building principals will tell you that while on paper their authority may look fairly impressive, in reality it is limited by the power of the teachers' unions and the informal norms of American education, according to which the classroom is the teacher's castle. Contrary to the image created by many public school critics, the delivery of educational products in American public schools is controlled not by a cabal of bureaucrats but by millions of teachers, all of whom consider themselves to be major authorities on educational practices. Compared to France, Germany, or Japan, the American public school system is radically decentralized, teacher-driven, and wondrously chaotic.

Notwithstanding the above, American public schools often resemble one another, not because of monopolistic practices, but because they represent the middle-class values that are enshrined in the public culture. Hard work, dependability, and respectability are the principles by which official school cultures are created. But those who have worked in schools also know that the official curriculum must compete with the student culture, which approaches learning with a certain indifference and holds respectability up as a kind of comic facade. American students do not accept authority lightly. The idea that they are victims of a state-monopolized curriculum and pedagogy is so out of keeping with reality that it borders on the ridiculous. Some of our students may be illiterate, and some may be subservient to their teachers, but a visit to any public school should quickly disabuse researchers of the notion that the state's monopoly of education is destroying students' spirits. What is keeping students from realizing their intellectual, artistic, and personal development are those cultural norms that elevate material acquisition over intellectual curiosity. The confusion between cultural uniformity and monopolistic practices has disoriented much of the discussion about school choice because much of the literature related to school choice does not sufficiently acknowledge that most American schools, public and private, are expressions of the dominant American culture, for better or worse.

The Proximate Causes of the School Choice Movement

The well of disappointment about public education was far deeper in the early 1980s than most liberals imagined. Public education was pictured in the media as top-heavy, bureaucratic, and incompetent; moreover, the ideal of integration was threatened by continuing racial segregation. To understand school choice, it is important to return to *Brown v. Board of Education*. In 1954, the Supreme Court ruled that racial segregation could not be constitutionally supported on the basis of the "separate but equal" principle indicated in *Plessy v. Ferguson* (1896). In effect, the Court found that separate was not equal and that minority students in the United States were being deprived of their right of equal protection under the law. The *Brown* decision radically altered American public education. In fact, the first choice schools were "white flight" academies. In their panic to avoid sending their children to school with African-American students, white parents throughout the South withdrew from the public school system and established private academies that were often indirectly publicly funded. *Brown*, however, spoke to an even deeper American dilemma by mandating that public schools be racially integrated; it implicitly called for the redesign of American education. Despite the Court's decision, de facto segregation continued, north and south, because America's neighborhoods are segregated by race and class.

By the 1960s it was becoming increasingly apparent that de facto segregation was, in the words of the Kerner Commission, creating two societies, one poor and minority, the other white and relatively affluent.

Numerous studies called for the reform of public education in the inner cities, and several articulate critics testified to the damage public education was doing to minority students. Jonathan Kozol, in particular, mapped out the terrain of pain with startling clarity. Moreover, writers such as Michael Harrington (1962) showed Americans that poverty continued to exist throughout the country. When Lyndon Johnson became President, he sought to build the "Great Society" by creating an environment of equal opportunity, material abundance, and social justice. Along with Rev. Martin Luther King, Jr., Johnson and other liberals attempted to integrate the country through court decision and legislation. The passions aroused by the war in Vietnam effectively destroyed the political consensus required to make the Great Society a reality. Moreover, the black power movement challenged the integrationist ideal by arguing for separation of the races and for racial pride. The objective was to gain control of the schools in black communities so that they could teach African-American–centered curricula and the values of the local community. In the minds of black power advocates, public schools were little more than extensions of white power, white ideology, and white control. To make matters more confusing, a number of white educational reformers continued to criticize the public school system as morally and intellectually deadening. Many of these critics formed alternative schools in New York and other major cities. As we will see shortly, the alternative-school movement was one of the seeds from which the school choice movement grew.

In the meantime, the economist Milton Friedman (1962) was arguing that by its very nature public education was an affront to the ideals of freedom and marketplace accountability. In essence, Friedman laid the groundwork for an alternative model of school governance that emphasized parental choice and the belief that markets are better arbiters of personal and social good than are state-mandated regulations. During the 1960s, however, Friedman was a lone voice in the policy wilderness. The core consensus was frayed, but still intact. However, he played a critical role in establishing the ideological credibility of Adam Smith's notion of the invisible hand guiding public policy.

We should also keep in mind that public education in the 1970s was quite experimental. In particular, the open classroom was idealized and new curricula such as "Man: A Course of Study" were touted as helping students to grasp the structure of knowledge through "discovery" learning. Teachers' unions, particularly under the leadership of Albert Shanker, became increasingly powerful. Public education seemed to be entering an era of optimism and there was a deep belief in experimentation in those public schools that had the resources to innovate. This sense of relative well-being, however, stood in stark contrast to the continuing educational disaster within the inner city. In particular, forced busing in cities like Boston created racial confrontations that were often violent. Anthony Lukas, in *Common Ground* (1986), documents the trauma of forced busing in Boston. Public education was increasingly politicized and conservatives, in particular, began to question the viability and advisability of using a public school system as an instrument of court-mandated racial integration. In effect, a politics of resentment developed against the liberal core consensus. It was not until 1980, however, that this underground current of hostility broke through the surface of politics as usual; the conservative coalition led by Ronald Reagan challenged the core consensus by arguing against state power and for market power. The ideas of Milton Friedman emerged from the back offices of policy think tanks to take their place in the Oval Office.

Crystallization and Intensification: School Choice Comes of Age

We have already noted that the reform movements of the 1980s had little effect on the overall redesign of American education and that the public school system was battered politically, particularly from the right. With the election of Reagan, the right gained the political power and the platform to wage war against liberal reforms. The new-right conservatives were joined in this struggle by a wide variety of Protestant evangelicals, who characterized public schools as repositories of secular humanism. Highly motivated politically, most evangelicals supported Reagan with a fervor that was just this side of a holy war. They gained informal and formal power in national politics and found new allies in such places as the U.S. Department of Education. During the 1980s, the department shifted its emphasis away from public education and tilted distinctly toward private education and school choice. Virtually all Republican secretaries of education were conservative supporters of school choice, and the most recent one, Lamar Alexander, publicly championed choice without reservation.

The establishment of the Center for Choice in Education within the Department of Education represented the institutionalization of the evangelical impulse and the open acknowledgment of conservative educational causes. Many of the publications the center distributes originate in the Heritage Foundation and other conservative think tanks. One wonders why the federal government is distributing the *Phyllis Schlafly Report*, the personal newsletter of a woman known for her far-right views. Through the Office of Research and Improvement, the department issued a booklet entitled *Getting Started—How Choice Can Renew Your Public Schools* (1992). The foreword to this document is by Diane Ravitch, a former assistant secretary of education. The center also distributes the work of Joe Nathan, a public school choice pioneer, and of Mary Anne Raywid, an educational philosopher and long-time choice advocate. Also available from the Center for Choice in Education is the literature issued by the Institute for Responsive Education, headed by Evans Clinchy, and several reports published by the Massachusetts Office of Educational Equity, directed by Charles Glenn. The above-mentioned names represent some of the guiding forces of school choice. Their "official" presence at the department demonstrates how intertwined the federal government has become with these special-interest advocates. "Civil Rights and Parental Choice," a report written by the libertarian lawyer Clint Bolick for the Department of Education, concluded that school choice was "every American's birthright—every American's *civil* right" (Bolick 1992:24).

The Department of Education is only one of many Washington-based public policy centers and institutes. Some of these centers have created what amounts to a conservative infrastructure which promotes market solutions to public problems. The Landmark Legal Foundation, a conservative public-interest law firm, for instance, has involved itself in several lawsuits concerning what its members believe to be state infringement on individual freedoms in the areas of public housing, economic liberties, and education.

According to Debra Cruel, a former attorney with Landmark, "People long to be noble and nobility is self-governance." She believes that intrinsically American values are slipping away and that people want to be "free—without restraints." The Landmark Legal Foundation also believes that the poor must lead a movement for individual liberation. An African-American, Cruel takes the position that traditional liberalism has failed to provide equal opportunity for minorities. A small but vocal number of African-Americans have come to question the efficacy of legislated equity. (This topic will be discussed in more depth in chapter 3, as it relates to the Milwaukee voucher experiment.) Besides the Landmark Legal Foundation, other conservative advocacy groups such as the Heritage Foundation have showered the media with studies and policy papers creating the impression that choice is highly desired by the American people and is a superior method for reforming schools. As we will see in chapter 4, much of this evidence is questionable.

The Washington lobbying infrastructure includes a variety of private school organizations that are strong advocates of school choice. Prominent among them are the National Association of Independent Schools (NAIS) and the Council for American Private Education. These groups have forged a collaboration with a number of religious and other private education groups, called the National Coalition for the Improvement and Reform of American Education. That most members of the coalition represent religious organizations tells us a great deal about the politics of private school choice. The members include Agudath Israel of America, the American Montessori Society, the Association of Military Colleges and Schools of the United States, Catholic Daughters of America, Catholic Golden Age, Christian Schools International, the Evangelical Lutheran Education Association, the Friends Council on Education, the Institute for Independent Education, the Jesuit Secondary Education Association, the Knights of Columbus, the National Association of Episcopal Schools, the National Association of Private Schools for Exceptional Children, the National Catholic Educational Association, the National Council on Catholic Women, the National Society of Hebrew Day Schools, the Seventh Day Adventist Office of Education, and the United States Catholic Conference (Walsh 1992:23).

Only very recently have private schools attempted to exert political power at the national level on behalf of some choice system. There are many reasons for this, but certainly the most significant is that many private schools are in a precarious financial situation and subsidized voucher programs would enable them to remain open. The viability of many Catholic schools in particular is questionable. In 1992 the Roman Catholic church undertook a mammoth publicity campaign, called "Discover Catholic School 1992." Nationwide, each of the church's 7,291 elementary schools and 1,296 high schools were asked to sell "an array of buttons, T shirts, pins, decals, posters, videos and banners that bear the logo of a proud galleon slicing through the waves, its sail emblazoned with a giant cross" (Allis 1991:48). Moreover, a variety of studies indicating that Catholic schools are superior to public schools in terms of student learning have been integrated into the policy literature and popular press. Nevertheless, Roman Catholic schools have suffered a dramatic enrollment decline—a 46 percent drop in students and a 29 percent drop in schools between the 1960s and the early 1980s (Erickson 1986:86). This trend has continued. At the same time that Catholic schools are suffering significant enrollment declines, other religious schools have been enjoying huge increases. For instance, the number of students in evangelical schools jumped by 627 percent, American Lutheran church schools grew 256 percent, and conservative Jewish schools grew 254 percent (Erickson 1986:87).

In the struggle to capture the minds, hearts, and votes of Americans, the school choice coalition also has been aided by think tanks, interest groups, and individuals who are not based in Washington and do not approach school choice from a religious or other private-school perspective. One of the most prominent and intellectually respected of these advocacy groups is the Manhattan Institute. It has released several studies about the benefits of school choice for poor, inner-city minority children. As we shall see, an examination of these data reveals that much of their evidence is unconvincing. Nonetheless, the Manhattan Institute continues to advocate school choice and is led by some of the country's most prominent banking and corporate executives, university professors, and Republican politicians, as well as a sprinkling of public school administrators and labor leaders. The institute's advisory board reads like a mini–*Who's Who* of the educational and business elite that constitutes the inner circle of the market-oriented school choice movement: Peter Flanigan (managing director, Dillon Read and Co.), Raymond Chambers (chairman, Wesray Capital Corp.), Linda Chavez (senior fellow, Manhattan Institute), John Chubb (founding member, Edison Project), James Coleman (professor of sociology, University of Chicago), A. Wright Elliott (executive vice president, Chase Manhattan Bank), Chester E. Finn, Jr. (founding member, Edison Project), Seymour Fliegel (former deputy superintendent, New York City Community School District 4), Colman Genn (superintendent, New York City Community School District 27), Richard Gilder, Jr. (partner, Gilder, Gagnon, and Co.), Nathan Glazer (professor of education, Harvard University), the Hon. Thomas Kean (president, Drew University), Joe Nathan (senior fellow, Humphrey Institute), Robert S. Peterkin (superintendent, Milwaukee Public Schools), Mary Anne Raywid (professor of education, Hofstra University), and Adam Urbanski (president, Rochester Teachers Association) (Domanico 1991).

However, support for school choice runs far deeper politically than the Washington and New York lobbying establishment. There is virtually no state in the Union in which grass-roots choice organizers have not made their impact on legislative and political processes. We will discuss the nature of the choice legislation that has been introduced throughout the country in chapter 3. Suffice it to say here that without the political pressure that has been brought to bear in each of these states, it is doubtful that these initiatives would have reached the floor of the legislatures. Choice initiatives have touched off ferocious political debates. In Pennsylvania, for instance, the battle for a choice bill was led by the Road to Educational Achievement through Choice (REACH), a coalition headed by the Pennsylvania Catholic Conference. Pitted against the 1991 choice bill was a coalition of twenty organizations led by the state teachers unions, the League of Women Voters, and the American Civil Liberties Union. Observers indicated that the school choice debate in Pennsylvania was even more vitriolic than the controversy that surrounded the legislature's passage of a restrictive abortion law. Threats and counterthreats were exchanged, and, according to one observer, "it was very hardball" (Diegmueller 1992).

Market-oriented reformers draw ideological support from a group of young conservative thinkers who are extremely well placed in the Republican party. These are the advocates of self-help, or the "New Paradigm"—actually a very old paradigm, whose origins can be traced to the market philosophy of Adam Smith. Essentially, the New Paradigm hypothesizes that state intervention to resolve social problems in fact creates more problems because it robs individuals of their freedom of choice, their integrity, and their capacity to influence markets as consumers. A representative of this New Paradigm is Chester E. Finn, Jr., who was called the Bush administration's "education philosopher—and the chief architect of Bush's master plan for fixing schools." Arguing that the "race is to the swift," Finn backs public funding for private schools and believes that competition with private schools will improve public schools. He goes so far as to imply that there is something unpatriotic about opposing private school vouchers: "It is un-American to force students to go to schools that they don't want to attend" (Toch 1991:46).

Choice made its first major national political breakthrough at the National Governors' Conference in 1986. In their report, *Time for Results*, the governors said, "If we first implement choice, true choice among public schools, we unlock the values of competition in the marketplace. Schools that compete for students, teachers, and dollars will, by virtue of the environment, make those changes that will allow them to succeed" (Paulu 1989:14). Three years later the White House held a workshop on school choice. President Bush spoke to the conference in near-reverential terms: "The evidence is striking and abundant. Almost without exception, wherever choice has been attempted—Minnesota, East Harlem, San Francisco, Los Angeles, and a hundred other places in between—choice has worked. . . . Bad schools get better. Good ones get better still, entire school systems have been restored to public confidence by the implementation of these choice plans. Disaffected families have been brought from private schools back into public education. Any school reform that can boast such success deserves our attention, our emphases, and our effort" (25–26). The future secretary of education, Lamar Alexander, also spoke about school choice: "The fact that so many people have come together . . . shows that this movement is kind of beyond all of us. It is bigger than all of us. It will keep going on after us, but perhaps we can do something to nurture it, and that is what we are all here for today" (25). Dennis Doyle, a senior research fellow at the Hudson Institute in Washington, D.C., and a workshop participant, summarized: "There is in the popular mind a vision of cut-throat competition, of profit- taking buccaneers, swashbuckling across the State, people who are . . . merciless, kind of Atlas Shrugged/Ayn Rand types. Well, there certainly is that type of competition, but there is competition which is closer to home . . . and that is the competition which emphasizes the supremacy of the consumer, consumer sovereignty, and that, in fact, is what competition is all about" (14). Apparently, this deep faith in the marketplace was substantiated for those attending the workshop by fourteen-year-old André Lawrence, who testified, "I was very happy to decide which school I wanted to attend. It was like shopping, buying a pair of shoes, shopping around until you find something you like" (14).

The workshop participants concluded that there was virtually no educational problem that could not be solved by choice and that choice produces at least eight benefits (Paulu 1989:11–24):

1. Choice can bring basic structural change to our schools.

2. Schools of choice recognize individuality.

3. Choice fosters competition and accountability.

4. Choice can improve educational outcomes.

5. Schools of choice can keep potential dropouts in school and draw back those who have already left.

6. Schools of choice increase parents' freedom.

7. Choice plans increase parent satisfaction and involvement in the schools.

8. Schools of choice can enhance educational opportunities, particularly for disadvantaged parents.

President Bush included several provisions for school choice in his plan for reforming education called "America 2000." This proposal included a two-million-dollar education certificate support fund and a thirty-million-dollar fund for creating "National School Choice Demonstration Projects." If, however, one had to choose a single document that captured the imagination of the choice movement and legitimated the idea of school choice to the news media and, hence to the public at large, it would have to be *Politics, Markets, and American Schools* by the political scientists John E. Chubb and Terry M. Moe. We will discuss the findings of these authors in detail in chapter 4. Essentially, Chubb and Moe believe that the natural operations of markets will drive out bad schools and reward good schools. They maintain that "markets offer an institutional alternative to direct democratic control," adding, "Without being too literal about it, we think that reformers would do well to entertain the notion that choice *is* a panacea. . . . Choice is a self-contained reform with its own rationale and justification. It has the capacity *all by itself* to bring about the kind of transformation that, for years, reformers have been seeking to engineer in myriad other ways. Indeed, if choice is to work to greatest advantage, it must be adopted *without* these other reforms, since the latter are predicted on democratic control and are implemented by bureaucratic means (1990:167, 217). Chubb and Moe address the question, Why are markets so effective? "A market system is not built to enable the imposition of higher-order values on the schools, nor is it driven by a democratic struggle to exercise public authority. Instead, the authority to make educational choices is radically decentralized to those most immediately involved. Schools compete for the support of parents and students, and parents and students are free to choose among schools. The system is built around decentralization, competition, and choice" (189).

By 1990, choice had won the moral and research high ground. A significant national movement had emerged beyond the Washington Beltway. Choice had caught the imagination of educational reporters; it was and is front-page news. Politicians saw choice as a way of reforming education without spending much money; choice also seemed to resonate with a cultural milieu that placed consumership at the center of the good life.

Voice, Exit, and Reform

We have examined how the school choice movement arose and entertained some speculations about why it did so in the 1980s. I have suggested that school choice is similar to a social issue. The 1980s were a time when markets seemed to triumph and individuals did not have to feel guilty about feathering their own nests. Privatization was and is a social policy and a cultural movement. The middle class, in particular, increasingly withdrew their support from public institutions, choosing "exit" over "voice" as a way of maximizing their interests (Hirschman 1970). By abandoning public institutions, the middle class could no longer influence public policy or participate in shaping the public agenda. The emphasis on the marketplace fed into a belief system in which a commodification of life seemed compatible with the good life. At the same time massive immigration from South America, Eastern Europe, and the Caribbean pressured the middle class to create their own educational enclaves. The fundamentalists were repelled by secular humanism and by a public school system that seemed to have lost faith with basic values. The melting-pot ideal that had animated belief in public education slipped from public consciousness, so that collective responsibilities were easy to deny. A large number of school choice lobbying groups arose throughout the country and placed the issue on the policy agenda. This is the stage upon which the school choice drama was set.

3 The Varieties of School Choice

How widespread is school choice in terms of legislation, and what does it look like where it has been implemented? It is my hope that this chapter will enable the reader to understand the diversity of school choice and to recognize that different choice policies have dramatically different effects on the redesign of American education.

Choice Legislation

In researching this book, I surveyed all fifty states to determine whether school choice policies had been proposed or enacted. The results of this survey appear in the Appendix. There is little doubt that the idea of choice has become increasingly popular. In 1988 Minnesota, which has traditionally been in the forefront of the alternative-schools movement, initiated a groundbreaking statewide choice program. Of course, Minnesota is unusual because it is relatively homogeneous demographically, and if its record in presidential elections is any indication, it may be the most politically liberal state in the Union. In 1989, however, Arkansas, Iowa, Nebraska, and Ohio also adopted choice plans; by 1991 ten states had approved some form of choice legislation. As of late 1992, some kind of choice legislation had been introduced in thirty-seven states. The most common forms of legislation are voucher proposals and interdistrict open-enrollment proposals. Choice is extremely popular in the Midwest. Republican governors tend to favor choice a bit more than their Democratic counterparts. The reason is not hard to see: Democratic governors tend to depend on teachers' unions for electoral support, and teachers' unions have almost universally opposed choice. In general, Democrats still support public institutions and remain loyal to the core consensus, while Republicans are more apt to favor market solutions for social problems.

There is very little school choice in the South, which is ironic because the South originated the concept of freedom of choice in education. In the 1960s choice was a way of maintaining segregated schools; in the 1990s it can be a mechanism for truly integrating schools. The northeastern United States has not been a hotbed of school choice legislation, although many local plans are quite successful. Most recently, a choice initiative was defeated in the Pennsylvania House of Representatives. Choice has not had a great impact in the West either, although there are strong movements in Colorado and Utah. In states that are thinly populated and where towns are separated by great distances, there are obvious practical limitations to how much choice parents and students can exercise. The West Coast, on the other hand, has been very active in the choice movement; in Oregon and California, in particular, voucher proposals have aroused a great deal of public controversy. There are no choice plans in Hawaii or Alaska.

Clearly, choice as a legislative movement does not lend itself to easy summary, and the success of choice legislation depends a great deal on the demographic and political characteristics of the particular state in which it is introduced. It is not surprising, for instance, that school choice is primarily a midwestern movement, since that region is quite homogeneous in terms of race and students crossing district lines there are not likely to change significantly the racial composition of schools. Yet it would be a mistake to argue that school choice is essentially a regional phenomenon. Advocates have long been active throughout the country.

The U.S. Department of Education publishes regular updates on developments in the field. The April 24, 1992, update included the following items:

Arizona: Senator Patterson introduced a new choice bill including private schools. Previously the Senator had introduced only public-school open-enrollment legislation. Also, the choice provisions of Governor Symington's education task force proposals were introduced as HB 2548.

Arkansas: A new citizens group, Arkansans for Better Education, is being formed with the goal of getting a school-voucher initiative on the state ballot in either 1992 or 1994.

California: The EXCEL (Excellence Through Choice in Education League) coalition continues to gather signatures to place the choice initiative on the November ballot.

Connecticut: On March 13, the Education Committee of the Connecticut Assembly held a hearing on charter-school recommendations embodied in AB 323, a bill to implement the findings of the Charter Schools Task Force created by the legislature in 1991. The Task Force issued its report on February 21, and recommended the establishment of six charter schools in the state on a pilot basis, beginning in 1994.

Florida: A pilot plan for at-risk children was narrowly defeated on March 13 by the Florida House. The proposal was offered as an amendment to a technical bill by Reps. Tom Feeney and Carlos Valdes and lost by only three votes. This was the first recorded vote in the Florida legislature on a voucher-type plan.

Kansas: A comprehensive statewide voucher bill, titled the "G.I. Bill for Children," was introduced by Senator Eric Yost and others as SB 633. The proposal is an expansion of Yost's SB 199, introduced in

1991. Both bills failed to meet the March 6 deadline for reporting new legislation and thus are not eligible for further consideration this year. However, either proposal could be offered as an amendment to other pending legislation.

Kentucky: On March 4 a group of Kentucky parents filed suit seeking tuition vouchers to enable them to choose religious schools for their children. The parents are alleging that their free exercise of religion is burdened by the requirement that they pay tax monies to support compulsory public schools which teach values that are not in keeping with their religion.

New Jersey: On February 13 Assembly Democratic Leader (and former speaker) Joseph Doria introduced a comprehensive school choice bill including a statewide open-enrollment program (interdistrict) as well as a voucher-type program to facilitate attendance at any nonpublic school. On April 8, New Jersey Citizens for a Sound Economy held a seminar on choice, at which Assemblymen Doria (D) and Dick Kamia (R) and others spoke.

Tennessee: On April 7 the Tennessee House Education Committee heard testimony on behalf of charter-school legislation backed by the Tennessee Parent Power Committee. The Committee voted to refer the charter-school bill to the Joint Education Oversight Committee for study. The next day, the Senate Education Committee held a hearing on charter schools, and also referred it for further study.

Texas: On April 15, James Leininger and other business leaders announced a $1.5-million scholarship program for low-income families. Their program was inspired by the privately funded voucher plan established by Pat Rooney and his Golden Rule Insurance Co. in Indianapolis.

Vermont: On March 4, the Senate Education Committee held a hearing on a resolution by its chair, Jeb Spaulding, and co-chair, John McClaughry, calling for a study of expanding choice in Vermont. The resolution subsequently passed the Senate. (U.S. Department of Education 1992:1–2)

What is apparent from these brief summaries is that school choice movements in every state are quite individual; moreover, each state's choice coalition has a unique political configuration. Usually, this configuration is drawn together by grass-roots choice movements, which are often backed by major businesses. In Illinois, for instance, the choice coalition is called TEACH (Taxpayers for Education Accountability and Choice); in Pennsylvania, the coalition is REACH (Road to Educational Achievement through Choice); in Arizona, the coalition is called PACE (Parents Advocating Choice in Education). Other groups include Floridians for Educational Choice, Oregonians for Educational Choice, and the Tennessee Parent Power Program. These groups come to Washington, D.C., regularly, where the Center for Choice in Education sponsors brown-bag lunch seminars. A favorite speaker is Pat Rooney of the Golden Rule Insurance Company, who initiated a privately funded voucher program in Indianapolis, and Bob Woodson, president of the National Center for Neighborhood Enterprise.

As governor of Arkansas, President Clinton was a strong supporter of public school choice, although his administration probably will not promote private school choice at the national level. In any case, it should be apparent that the issue of choice has moved onto the legislative battlefield. What can we learn about choice as it already exists? In the next section we examine six case studies. As we shall see, each not only represents one of the varieties of school choice but also grounds the choice controversy in a particular sociological environment.

The Spirit of Minnesota

Joe Nathan is an educational innovator who was instrumental in starting the choice movement in Minnesota. He was involved in the creation of the St. Paul Open School and is a relentless critic of what he perceives as the oppressiveness of much of public education. Currently director of the Center for School Change at the Hubert H. Humphrey Institute of Public

Affairs of the University of Minnesota, Nathan has worked for the National Governors' Association and was an educational consultant to the Bush administration. He writes a weekly education column for the *St. Paul Pioneer Press* and has published several books on school choice. He came of age intellectually in the 1960s and honed his educational and political skills in the alternative-schools movement. Nathan was active in the civil rights movement and sees educational liberty as a matter of civil rights. In essence, he represents what might be thought of as the progressive wing of the school choice movement.

It is sometimes difficult to remember that American progressivism began in the Midwest. The populist philosophy of the Progressive party of Robert La Follette had its origins in midwestern radicalism, and Eugene Debs, the presidential candidate of the American Socialist party, was also a midwesterner. During the 1920s midwestern farmers were radicalized, and their representatives in Congress attempted to pass a series of farm subsidy programs that were as socialistic as any legislation that has ever been introduced at the national level. John Dewey was a midwesterner and did most of his work in Kansas, Iowa, and Michigan before he came to Columbia University.

Minnesotans are particularly progressive — a rare combination of radical individualism and social consciousness. School choice is in the soil of the state's political culture, but what caused it to bear fruit was a personal experience of Rudy Perpich, a Democrat who moved with his family to St. Paul in the 1970s, when he was elected lieutenant governor. The Perpichs were not satisfied with the school their daughter was assigned to, but they discovered that by law she could not attend a public school outside her district. Outraged, Perpich organized a coalition of legislators who were interested in parental choice and were supported by the Minnesota Business Partnership. Minnesota had already implemented tuition tax deductions for parents who sent their children to private school. This legislation was first enacted in 1958 and was later upheld by the U.S. Supreme Court in the 1983 *Mueller v. Allen* case. When Perpich became governor in 1976, he and his colleagues created a smorgasbord of school choice options as part of a nine-part "access to excellence" program. The initial choice wedge was the postsecondary options plan, in which eleventh- and twelfth-grade students were given an opportunity to take college courses for high school credit. In 1990 some fifty-seven hundred students took advantage of the program. The real goal of Perpich and the radical Minnesota school redesigners, however, was a statewide open-enrollment policy that would essentially destroy what they believed was a public school monopoly. It is not surprising, therefore, that Perpich was opposed by most educational establishment leaders in the state.

Although geographically large, politically Minnesota feels like a small town. Ted Kolderie, a public policy analyst who puts out a regular newsletter and is a strong believer in charter schools, introduced me to the political culture that surrounds school choice in Minnesota. I accompanied Kolderie to a meeting in a suburb of Minneapolis where a group of teachers were trying to convince the school board that they ought to be allowed to start a charter school. The micro-politics of this meeting were fascinating. The essential issue was whether public education would remain in the hands of publicly elected officials, such as the school board, or would be at least partially privatized, with some control passing to teachers and parents. If the public school abolitionists in Minnesota have their way, public education will simply disappear because radical deregulation and decentralization will remove control from elected officials and place it in the hands of a multitude of small, autonomous groups. Charter schools are only one element of the choice options available in Minnesota. In addition to the postsecondary enrollment plan mentioned above, the state offers several other options:

- The Open Enrollment Program allows students in kindergarten through twelfth grade to attend a school outside the district in which they live. The High School Graduation Incentives Program is designed for students who are not likely to graduate or who have dropped out of school before getting their diploma. These students may choose from a variety of education options to complete the requirements needed to graduate.

- Diploma Opportunities for Adults Aged Twenty-one and Over gives qualified learners who have not completed high school up to two years of free state aid to return to finish their requirements.

- Area Learning Centers offer personalized education programs year-round, day and evening, to accommodate learners from age twelve through adult. A wide variety of courses leading to diplomas are taught, using alternate methods of instruction. Additional services are provided to assure each learner's success.

- Public or Private Alternative Programs personalize the education of learners who are at risk of not completing high school. Classes are taught using alternative methods and flexible scheduling.

- Education Programs for Pregnant Minors and Minor Parents are designed to encourage parenting and pregnant teens to continue their education and receive their high school diplomas.

As this list indicates, there is no shortage of school choice ideas in Minnesota, and there is little doubt that these enrollment options have redesigned education in the state. Yet, surprisingly, fewer students participate in these programs than might be expected given the programs' political high profiles and the publicity that has surrounded the Minnesota reforms. In the school year 1989–1990, for instance, less than one-half percent of Minnesota students participated in the open-enrollment option. According to a report issued by Joe Nathan and Wayne Jennings (1990), significant numbers of students participating in some form of school choice come from low-income families. While this report makes glowing claims of student success, one must be skeptical, given that the number of students involved is relatively small. In fact, the data are strikingly weak in documenting improved learning opportunities for the participants. Somehow, the ideological enthusiasm surrounding the choice movement in Minnesota has not resulted in the educational transformation its advocates envisioned. Moreover, there is evidence that some small rural schools have suffered declining enrollments and thus have had to cut their educational offerings. Opponents of school choice in Minnesota sometimes claim that school choice is elitist and that wealthy suburban districts exclude low-income and minority students from nearby cities.

The enrollment options in Minnesota, therefore, have not been very effective in transforming public or private education. This is not to say that specific students have not benefited or that certain schools have not been improved as a result of the market incentives provided by open-enrollment policies. But the fact remains that most students continue to attend their local public school and that many of the enrollment options that are so highly touted are rather marginal to the overall educational enterprise in the state. Choice advocates often argue that open-enrollment policies have secondary effects, meaning that competition leads to school improvement even if the number of students choosing non-neighborhood schools is relatively small. But is this indirect method of reforming schools really the best method? This leads one to wonder whether charter schools are as much a breakthrough issue as some have thought.

In 1991 the Minnesota legislature passed a provision that would permit licensed teachers to create innovative schools, essentially on contract to a public school board. These charter schools may be redesigned existing schools or new schools. As mentioned earlier, the charter schools are accountable to public authority as well as to parents. Advocates of charter schools believe that the contract idea will increase educational accountability. The idea was originally suggested by Albert Shanker of the American Federation of Teachers in a speech to the National Press Club in March 1988. Later Shanker gave essentially the same speech at the Itasca Seminar, a retreat sponsored by the Minneapolis Foundation. Minnesota has a long history of school-site management and contract schools. In essence, charter schools will be public schools that have some of the characteristics of private schools. Deeply embedded in the charter school concept is the assumption schools chosen by students and families are more accountable and, thus, better learning environments. As we shall see, this assumption, which is the policy equivalent of a choice mantra, may be unfounded. Moreover, while certain charter schools may be successful, it is difficult to believe that any large-scale system of charter schools could produce a coherent system of public education.

The alternative-schools model of school choice may ignore real issues of accountability. In fact, issues of social stratification, while burning in the rhetoric of the educational innovators, are singularly lacking in their program design. The balance between liberty and equity in Minnesota will be radically altered if the entire public school system is deregulated. Rhetoric aside, there is little indication that educational choice has led to greater equality of opportunity for the school-age children of the state.

A Tale of Two Schools

Choice advocates often cite certain exemplary schools as evidence of the success of open-enrollment policies. Yet the definition of choice can be highly eclectic, and very often the issue of cause and effect is badly muddled: Does a school become productive because it is a choice school, or do productive schools attract a wider range of families? And to what degree is an exemplary choice school the result of a charismatic principal, a uniquely configured faculty, or unusual resources? Two schools in Minnesota, the Miltona Science Magnet School and the Urban League Street Academy in St. Paul, represent two different worlds of choice. Miltona is in the heart of the farm country, while the Street Academy is in the midst of the inner-city ghetto.

Miltona is a tiny agricultural community two and a half hours northwest of Minneapolis. Agriculture in Minnesota is somewhat depressed, and in the past several years the state Board of Education has been encouraging small communities to consolidate their schools. This consolidation movement, however, has been resisted because small towns in Minnesota use their schools as community centers. Schools are often the focal points of the towns, and the citizens of the towns and the nearby farms take pride in the accomplishments of their schools and the students who attend them. According to Tom Andert, principal of the Miltona Magnet School, "School is the culture of the community."

During the period of consolidation, it looked as though the Miltona School might be closed, so Andert and a group of teachers wrote a proposal that turned the small elementary school into a science magnet school. Essentially, Miltona is a school of choice in a rather large geographic area and has attracted families because of its innovative curriculum, the centerpiece of which is its emphasis on science. The whole school feels a bit like a science lab and includes a weather station, a greenhouse, and innumerable child-made scientific instruments. According to Andert, most of the kids come from Norwegian farm families, with an orientation that he refers to as "Be nice to your neighbors." Interestingly, these families have progressive ideas about education and are supportive of what amounts to a progressive-school approach to teaching and learning. There is an air of informality and innovation at Miltona that would have made John Dewey feel at home.

But is the success of Miltona the product of school choice or the product of Andert, his fellow teachers, and the community in which they work? Andert and his colleagues have devised an elaborate strategy to bring parents into the school, which includes newsletters, radio announcements, open houses, and visits with teachers. This aspect of choice does seem to be related to school improvement. According to Andert, however, the parents are already motivated to take part in their children's education. Moreover, as I mentioned earlier, the school is the heart of the community. In fact, Andert is the mayor of the town.

The Urban League Street Academy is a privately organized alternative program that seeks to personalize the education of students at risk and enable them to complete high school. Located in the basement of an old building, the Street Academy, unlike Miltona, has not had a fresh coat of paint in years and has no funds for capital improvements. The principal, Perry Price, is an African-American educator who is struggling to create a learning environment, primarily for African-American students who have either dropped out of or been dismissed from public school. Seventy-five students are enrolled in the school; approximately forty-five attend on any given day. The curriculum is African-American—centered, with an emphasis on black literature. There are five teachers and a librarian and no substitute teachers, which means that if a teacher is absent, students have no teacher for the duration of the absence. The school relies primarily on donations for equipment, including paper and books, and there is a constant struggle to keep enough toilet paper in the restrooms and to keep the classrooms clean. Price needs psychological support for his students, and he needs lockers. At the Street Academy there is no place for students to hang up their coats. The library consists of inexpensive paperback books that have been lovingly catalogued.

To me, however, the visual experience that best symbolizes the stratification of educational opportunity is the science lab at the academy. Tucked away in a corner of the building, the lab consists of a counter punctuated by sinks and faucets. Underneath the counter are drain pipes that hang in mid-air; they lead nowhere because they are unconnected to a water main. The academy cannot afford to connect these pipes, so students cannot actually do science experiments; they can only pretend. When I compare the science room at the academy with the labs I have seen in suburban public schools and elite private schools, I cannot help but reflect on how unfairly we treat the poor children of this country. According to Price, he never turns down a student, but students do often get lost in the system.

The contrast between the Miltona Science Magnet School and the Urban League Street Academy is startling and disturbing. The academy was recommended to me by choice advocates in Minnesota as an example of how private alternatives to public education can meet the needs of at-risk students. I have little doubt that Perry Price is no less dedicated to his students and to his school than Tom Andert is. But without resources, all the school redesigning imaginable will be an empty exercise. Private alternatives to public education run the risk of creating a pseudo-solution that seems convincing on paper but, in reality, is no solution at all. School choice alone cannot solve social problems. The class and race divisions in American society are too deep to be bridged by student-enrollment policies. Moreover, change for change's sake can create a marketplace of educational boutiques where educational rhetoric and reality are blurred.

Bonnie Blodgett, who lives in St. Paul, recently wrote an article in *Lears* magazine about the complexity of choosing schools for her two daughters and asks some telling questions about the nature of what must be called incessant innovation in Minnesota. After a humorous description of her convoluted story, she asks, "Has the teaching profession learned nothing worth keeping over the centuries? Why don't teachers know whether having one's own desk is a good or a bad thing?" Blodgett discovered that most of the parents she came in contact with were disappointed in their own public school education. Choice seems to offer families alternatives that were previously unavailable. The metaphor for the Minnesota choice plan, according to Blodgett, is the shopping mall. Beneath the marketing hoopla lie questions of substance. Does choice alone create better schools? Or does it merely create schools that are better at marketing? Blodgett continued, "What did I want from the schools? Somewhat to my surprise, I was beginning to know. I wanted what I thought public education had always offered in America. I wanted a more or less level playing field, on which boys and girls could be trained to take up their places, whatever places their talents and affinities indicated, in the productive sphere and civic life of their country" (Blodgett 1992:54).

Is it not ironic that the redesigning of education in Minnesota has provided parents with every option except the one they want most: a strong, equitable, and productive public educational system that innovates with purpose, but retains a sense of cultural continuity that connects students and families to an educational heritage? Have the redesigners overstated their case?

A School Grows in East Harlem

The condition of urban education in the United States amounts to a national scandal. The schools that warehouse the poor inner-city children of this country are more like badly run prisons than educational institutions. The data concerning urban education have been flooding the newspapers and the television media for over a decade; yet, with some exceptions, the educational opportunities available to youngsters in the inner cities are becoming less and less attractive. At a time when many state legislatures are appropriating money to build prisons, they are cutting back appropriations for building schools—despite the fact that major cities are experiencing a new wave of immigration, not only from the Caribbean and South America, but from Asia and eastern Europe as well. School buildings are overcrowded to the point of bursting. In New York City, teachers and students use closets, anterooms to bathrooms, and hallways for instructional purposes.

In the late 1960s, New York City's public school system was broken up into thirty-two separate community school districts, each to be governed by an elected community school board and by the central Board of Education. High schools remained under the authority of the Board of Education. Decentralization brought with it the promise of community control, educational relevance, and the possibility that families would be able to transform schools in their own neighborhoods. Much of this promise was unfulfilled. Decentralization did not lead to an educational renaissance; in fact, there are widespread stories of corruption and patronage. Within this context, however, one community school district managed to create an educational oasis that has captured the public imagination and given hope to many that urban education is salvageable. The story of Community School District 4 in East Harlem has become a kind of educational epic. The flagship school of this reform movement, Central Park East Secondary School, is cited by choice advocates from Washington, D.C., to Los Angeles as an example of how choice can save urban education. Deborah Meier, the principal of Central Park East, is a winner of a MacArthur Foundation "genius" award and has written and spoken eloquently about the power of choice to transform schools. In this case study, we will examine the reform movement in Community School District 4, guided by two fundamental questions: What is the relationship between choice and charisma? And does choice precede innovation, or is it the other way around?

Poverty and Progressive Education
East Harlem epitomizes the plight of American inner cities. Its 113,000 residents live in a 2.2-square-mile area, twice the general population density of New York City. Its housing stock is in disrepair, which is a polite way of saying that a great deal of the community is simply crumbling. Twenty percent of the building lots are either vacant or occupied by abandoned buildings, and 27 percent of all residential buildings are classified as tenements. Thirty-five percent of the residents receive public assistance and, as of 1991, the median household income in the community was $8,300, the lowest of all communities in Manhattan. Twenty-five percent of the households are headed by a single female.

The district serves over 14,000 students: 60 percent Hispanic, 35 percent African-American, 4 percent white, and 1 percent Asian. Almost 80 percent of the students are eligible for free lunch programs because of their low-income status. Ten percent are classified as "limited English proficient" because they have scored below the twentieth percentile on a test of English-language ability. In 1974, only 15 percent of the students in the district could read above the level of the grade they were in; East Harlem ranked at the very bottom of all New York City school districts in reading achievement (Domanico 1989:4–6).

This was the educational situation when Anthony Alvarado became superintendent of schools in District 4 in 1974. That fall Alvarado began experimenting with alternative schools, including the East Harlem School for the Performing Arts. Essentially, Alvarado invited dynamic teachers to set up alternative schools, generally at the junior-high level. One of his major innovations was the minischool. Whereas previously each school building housed one school, Alvarado recognized that one building could house several schools. These schools were, in the words of Meier, the "brainchildren" of particular individuals or groups of teachers. Most of the schools were designed around curricular themes — science, environmental studies, performing arts, marine biology. Meier and her colleagues founded the Central Park East Secondary School, which enrolls students from grades seven through twelve and is affiliated with Theodore Sizer's Coalition of Essential Schools, a reform collaborative based on Sizer's theories of educational improvement. Staff members were volunteers, although all schools operated within the legal context established by the Board of Education, the New York State Regents, and the United Federation of Teachers. In 1980 all sixth-graders in the district were allowed to choose the junior high they wished to attend. Most elementary schools remained neighborhood schools.

The district operates a formal admissions process. Parents are given an information booklet about each of the junior highs in the district and can attend an orientation session at each of the schools. Once students and parents have been informed of their options, they fill out an application form ranking their choices from one through six. Students must also indicate in a brief statement why they chose the schools they did. There are no rules governing the procedures the junior high school staff may use in selecting its students, although no school may accept more than 20 percent of its entering class from outside the district's boundaries. Schools may review a child's academic record and may request a personal interview. Sixty percent of the students in the district are accepted into their first-choice school, 30 percent into their second-choice school, and 5 percent into their third-choice school. The remaining 5 percent are placed in schools that are thought to be most appropriate for them. We might note here that the argument that poor people do not know how to make educational choices for their children does not hold up in East Harlem. Parents are actively engaged in choosing schools for their children, and there is no indication that they are less aware of the alternatives open to them than other parents.

The policy of allowing teachers to found alternative schools has led to a great deal of educational diversity in District 4. These alternative schools include the Academy for Environmental Science, the Human Service School, the Creative Learning Community, the East Harlem School for Health and Biomedical Studies, the Isaac Newton School for Math and Science, New York Prep, the Rafael Cordero Bilingual School, and the José Feliciano Performing Arts School. It should be noted that many of these schools occupy the same building and that, despite their impressive names, the reality of these schools may be quite different than what is imagined by those who have come to romanticize District 4. Each school may have different class schedules, so that buzzers may be ringing almost continuously throughout the day. The buildings themselves may be quite dilapidated and resources scarce. Not all teachers in District 4 are inspirational; the district still has its share of time-servers and authoritarians. Reforming urban education takes more than dreams; it takes resources.

The most famous of the alternative schools in District 4 are those founded by Deborah Meier and her colleagues. Meier believes strongly that schools can serve as models for democratic life. According to her, "Creating a democratic community was both an operational and an inspirational goal. While we were in part the products of what was called 'open' education, our roots went back to early progressive traditions, with their focus on the building of a democratic community, on education for full citizenship and for egalitarian ideals. We looked upon Dewey, perhaps more than Piaget, as our mentor" (Meier 1987:36). When Alvarado, in 1974, asked Meier to start a school in one wing of P.S. 171, in essence she and her colleagues began a progressive school for poor children. Central Park East Secondary School reminds me of New York's Dalton School in the 1940s and 1950s. There is a minimum of administrators, the high school is divided into houses, each with its assigned faculty members, students stay with teachers for two years in a row, the faculty have a great deal to say about the nature of the curriculum, and there is an emphasis on writing.

The Senior Institute prepares students for graduation. In order to graduate, a student must complete fourteen portfolio areas, including traditional subjects such as math and history as well as an autobiography and a postgraduate plan. There is an emphasis on multicultural education and on having students interact, state their opinions, and give direction to their own education. Much has been written about the success of the Central Park East schools. It is true that, relative to other city schools, there is a very high graduation rate among the students, and that many graduates of the junior highs in the district go on to attend selective public secondary schools and prestigious private high schools. There is also some evidence that reading scores for the district have risen dramatically since choice was instituted. We will turn to these data in the next chapter as we review the evidence concerning the relationship between school choice and student achievement. There is little doubt that Meier and her colleagues have created a spirit of reform in East Harlem that has offered a glimmer of hope in an otherwise very sad picture of educational despair.

But the experiments in District 4 have not been widely copied throughout the New York metropolitan area, despite the fact that in 1992 former Schools Chancellor Joseph A. Fernandez instituted a citywide choice plan. Over time more families may make use of the choices available to them, and if this leads to the creation of smaller, more responsive schools, then the work that was begun in District 4 will improve schools throughout the city. Still, we might ask, was it choice or charisma that put the educational reforms in District 4 on the policy map? The publicity that has surrounded school reform in District 4 has created the aura of an educational spiritual revival. This atmosphere has made analysis difficult.

In the 1920s a group of researchers were hired by an industrialist to see how the labor force could be made more productive. The researchers found that the workers they studied were more productive than the workers they did not study. It was determined that the very fact of being observed made workers feel better about themselves and, thus, they became more productive. This is known as the Hawthorne effect, after the plant in which the research was located. Clearly, there is something of a Hawthorne effect going on in District 4. After all, the world is telling the students in the district schools that they have accomplished a great deal. It is little wonder that this positive feeling is reflected in students' attitudes. Moreover, District 4 has received a great deal of outside funding, which has made it possible to promote innovations. In sum, we can say that District 4 is a noble experiment in educational innovation, but not a good example of how choice alone can transform urban education. Change preceded choice in East Harlem, not the other way around (Harrington and Cookson 1992). As we will see, charismatic educators often promote choice for good cause, but in the process outsiders often confuse policy with personality and lose track of the relationship between cause and effect.

The Massachusetts Model

Thus far we have examined two very different types of school choice plans. In Minnesota, we examined a statewide choice plan that was predicated on an alternative-schools model. Essentially, the goal of the Minnesota plan is to redesign completely the way in which educational services are delivered. In this sense, Minnesota's plan challenges the core consensus about the relationship between school and society. East Harlem is an example of choice evolving almost by chance. It is localized in its impact, and the main thrust of educators there has been to create innovative schools, not to redesign urban education. Much of what has gone on in East Harlem is consistent with the core consensus that public education is the backbone of democracy.

We turn now to yet another model of school choice, called controlled choice. In this model student assignment policies are in good part determined by the racial composition of communities. Controlled choice is essentially a noncoercive method of achieving racial integration, first experimented with in Cambridge, Massachusetts. It is a choice program that is meant to redesign the way educational services are delivered, but firmly within the liberal tradition. In fact, controlled choice had its origins in the civil rights movement. In this section we examine the origins of controlled choice, its essential elements, and how it works in three communities: Cambridge and Fall River, Massachusetts, and White Plains, New York.

Genteel images of Massachusetts—Beacon Hill, Harvard University, the Boston Symphony—are somewhat deceptive. In reality, Massachusetts, especially Boston, is a multicultural, rock 'em–sock 'em political environment where the pendulum tends to swing from left to right on a yearly, sometimes monthly, basis. Anyone who has read Anthony Lukas's *Common Ground* (1986) knows that school politics in Massachusetts is high-stakes, emotional, and sometimes violent. Massachusetts is also the home state of some of the country's leading advocates of school choice. Stephen Arons, a law professor at the University of Massachusetts at Amherst, has long argued that compulsory education violates the freedom of expression guaranteed by the First Amendment. Prof. Charles L. Glenn of Boston University, former executive director of the Office of Educational Equity in the Massachusetts Department of Education, has been struggling for school choice since the 1970s. Harvard professor Charles V. Willie has cowritten many urban desegregation plans and has fought for educational justice throughout his career. Finally, Michael Alves, who worked in the state Office of Educational Equity and has been instrumental in establishing controlled-choice programs in Cambridge and several other Massachusetts towns, is also a consultant for controlled choice and helped design the program currently in place in White Plains. Twenty-five cities and towns in Massachusetts have opted for school choice, and the momentum for greater educational freedom of choice does not seem to be slowing.

The depth of feeling about educational justice among advocates for controlled choice is difficult to overstate. In Charles Glenn's office, for instance, there is a large picture of Abraham Lincoln. Perhaps I should not have been surprised when Glenn looked me in the eye and said, "You cannot have a school system half slave, half free." Glenn, a prolific writer and defender of controlled choice, has been publicly attacked by Abigail Thernstrom, an opponent of affirmative action and racial quotas (Thernstrom 1991:12,14). Essentially, Thernstrom wants complete freedom of choice and a voucher system. But Glenn has remained steady in his vision that education must provide minority (and other poor) children equal access to any public school (or publicly supported nonpublic school) on the same basis as other children. A minister with an educational mission, Glenn epitomizes the commitment to justice that animates so much of the controlled-choice movement.

Michael Alves is also a man with a mission. He advocated school choice "before the hype." He speaks of choice as an evolving innovation and is deeply committed to providing educational variety, as distinct from educational anarchy. Alves told me that in Boston and Cambridge the opposition to choice has been formidable because controlled choice breaks down the concept of the neighborhood school and at the same time seeks to integrate the schools. Alves's greatest concern is that the market wing of the school choice movement will triumph and that this will lead to resegregation. I asked him if the U.S. Department of Education had ever contacted him to discuss his experiences with controlled choice. I was surprised to learn that it had not, since in my trips to Washington, Cambridge had been cited innumerable times as an example of a city where choice works. Alves feels that during the Reagan and Bush administrations, the department was more interested in private school choice than in racial integration.

Originally, Massachusetts attempted to promote educational excellence and equity through the use of public magnet schools. The problem with such schools is that although they help some students, they have little impact on providing educational equity throughout a district. Under the leadership of Glenn and Alves, a controlled-choice plan was pioneered in Cambridge, a city composed primarily of well-educated, affluent college professors and a very poor African-American population. In controlled choice the automatic assignment of pupils to schools on the basis of where they live is abolished, and parents of children new to the school system or moving to the next level of schooling receive information about all options before indicating their preferences. Assignments are then made that satisfy these preferences so far as they are consistent with available capacities and local policies and requirements, which include desegregation. According to Glenn, controlled choice has four major objectives:

1. to give all pupils in a community equal access to every public school, not limited by where their families can afford to live;

2. to involve all parents (not just the most sophisticated) in making informed decisions about where their children will go to school;

3. to create pressure for the improvement, over time, of every school by eliminating guaranteed enrollment on the basis of residence; and

4. *where necessary,* to achieve racial desegregation of every school with as few mandatory assignments as possible (Glenn 1991:16).

To make controlled choice work, a truly effective parent information and outreach program is essential. The establishment of information centers in school districts that have instituted controlled choice has produced many positive outcomes, such as fostering a sense of community. According to Glenn, controlled choice should also include measures to ensure that real educational choices become available. This points to a key issue: Much of the discussion of school choice has focused on the demand side of choosing schools, but what of the supply side? What is the point of having a system of school choice where the choices are universally inadequate? Glenn argues that to transform education, it is necessary to remove bureaucratic obstacles to new approaches, to help schools that are not able to attract applicants, and to provide opportunities for teachers, parents, and others to initiate alternatives inside or outside of existing educational structures.

The Cambridge Experiment
In March 1991 the Cambridge School Committee adopted the final phase of its long-range school-desegregation plan. Since Cambridge has only one

public high school and no junior high or middle schools, the desegregation plan affected only those schools that enroll students from kindergarten to the eighth grade. All individual school attendance boundaries at the grade levels were abolished, and the alternate student assignment policy was aimed at "maximizing competition and choice among desegregated schools." Specifically, the assignment policy was designed:

1. to resolve a potential de jure segregation dispute with the Massachusetts Board of Education by reducing racial isolation and preventing resegregation among schools;

2. to provide for both stability of assignment and continuing desegregation with a minimum of mandatory student assignments;

3. to increase public support for desegregating urban schools by attracting and retaining more school-age children in the Cambridge public schools;

4. to provide enhanced educational opportunities for all students regardless of their race or socio-economic status (Alves and Willie 1987:91,92).

Ninety-one percent of all students entering the Cambridge public school system at the kindergarten through eighth-grade levels have gained admission to a school of their choice: 75 percent to the school of their first choice and 16 percent to either their second or third choice. Two factors account for this high rate of accommodation: families have multiple school choices, and Cambridge operates an extremely effective parent information and outreach program.

The heart of the Cambridge experiment is the Parent Information Center. Essentially, it operates as a community service organization that provides information to families about local elementary schools. Parent information centers serve multiple functions: they compel parents to think about their children's education, they provide information about the schools in the community, and they prod schools to improve and sharpen their missions. The Cambridge center provides printed literature describing the choice process and advising parents how to take advantage of it. Parents are encouraged to visit schools, and principals and faculties are encouraged to examine their curricula and educational philosophies. When I visited the center in Cambridge, I was impressed by the dignity surrounding the process and the care given to each family, no matter what its racial, ethnic, or socio-economic status. A key element in making choice work is that the system must have complete integrity—there can be no playing of favorites when it comes to accepting students into the schools of their choice.

Alves and Willie found that the controlled-choice experiment in Cambridge achieved its objectives in that there was no drift toward resegregation in the public schools and the system's desegregated schools have remained desegregated. Controlled choice is far more effective in achieving these goals than magnet schools or redistricting. After four years of controlled choice, it was found that minority students were outperforming white students in math and reading citywide. The attendance rate had risen 9 percent (Alves and Willie 1987:95–96).

Controlled choice is a desegregation technique that is particularly suited to cities with large minority populations because it builds on previous attempts to ensure quality integrated education. In the school districts I visited that have implemented controlled choice, there is a sense of enthusiasm and purpose that is often missing in American education. Unlike the alternative-schools or market models of choice, controlled choice is justice-driven, with an emphasis on equity. Ironically, this emphasis on equity and equal access has indirect educational-design ramifications that lead to school improvement without undermining or destroying public education. This conclusion is based on my observations not only in Cambridge, but also in Fall River and White Plains.

Fall River

Fall River is a small industrial and maritime city of approximately ninety thousand people, located in southeastern Massachusetts. During the nineteenth and early twentieth centuries, Fall River was an important center for the textile industry. By the 1960s the city had sunk into an economic depression from which it has only recently begun to recover. For many years the city has attracted immigrant Portuguese families, coming predominantly from the Azores, Portugal, and Brazil. Nearly 250 Portuguese families arrive in the city every year. There is also a recent wave of emigrants from Cambodia and South America. In the fall of 1987, the Fall River public schools embarked on an educational venture aimed at accomplishing two major goals: eliminating all vestiges of minority isolation in the schools and dramatically improving the education of all children. They instituted a controlled-choice plan very similar to that of Cambridge. Parents played a significant role in planning and implementing the choice program in Fall River. As in Cambridge, every school in Fall River is a magnet school and a school of choice. A citywide Parent Advisory Council was established, and parents throughout the city were surveyed about what kinds of educational options they would like to see for their children. A parent information and outreach system was established and an evaluation system designed to assess and track the plan's progress.

Thirty-eight percent of the Fall River parents who chose schools since the inception of this program have chosen non-neighborhood schools. Eighty-two percent of the students were admitted to their first-choice school, and 90 percent to one of their first two schools of choice. There is more racial balance in the schools than there was in the past, and the general educational renaissance in Fall River has been remarkable. Some of the breakthroughs have included literacy/media centers, adopt-a-school programs, mentor programs, computer-assisted education, a transitional bilingual-education program, special arts programs, a whole-language or literature-based approach to reading, and an environmental/marine science program. Part of the push toward school improvement in Fall River is the evolution of school-based management and the continuing pursuit of genuine diversity. Recently, there has been some discussion of expanding choice to other nearby suburban school districts.

Most parents visit the parent information center in February. They are asked to bring several documents, including the child's birth certificate and evidence of physical examination of the child by a physician. School assignments are based on space availability, the presence of a sibling in a particular school, linguistic minority balance, proximity of the school to home, and a random lottery. Every child receives a free book and an application for a library card as he or she leaves the center. The center exudes an air of enthusiasm and love for children—qualities that are personified by Fred Houle, the parent-community liaison, and Jim Wallace, the equal educational opportunity planner and desegregation coordinator. Clearly, these men are committed to public education and see choice as a way of achieving integration, but also as a way of revitalizing a community. According to Houle and Wallace, among the key benefits of a choice program are that parents become involved in their children's education and that schools are forced to institute improvements. They emphasize that choice in Fall River is a grass-roots program, not dependent on market models of educational reform. Families, they say, tend to "look at themselves in a different way when they choose schools." For Houle and Wallace, choice is evidence that democracy does work.

The outreach program in Fall River is extensive. It includes literature about each school participating in the choice program, contact with preschools, telephone surveys, direct mail, and a monthly newsletter called the *Magnet Memo*. Outreach is a key element in making controlled choice work. Another factor Houle and Wallace feel is critical in achieving the goals of equity and excellence is the support of a strong superintendent of schools who is able to build up a constituency for choice. When choice was being introduced in Fall River, the superintendent, other administrators, and teachers were out almost every night discussing choice with teachers, community groups, civic organizations, and community activists. Another key element in making choice work is to let the power flow to those who must own the choice program—the parents. Without parental involvement, choice cannot succeed. Last, it is extremely helpful to have some outside funding to finance parent information centers and other expenses related to school choice.

White Plains

Located some thirty minutes from New York City, White Plains has a highly diverse student population of approximately five thousand. Most of the white population lives in single-family housing in middle-class or upper-middle-class neighborhoods, while most of the minority population lives in subsidized housing projects. An increasing number of students come from homes where English is not the primary language, and the district educates scores of children from homeless families. In 1988, the Board of Education, with the encouragement of Saul M. Yanofsky, who since has become the superintendent of schools, approved an ambitious plan to restructure the entire district. Its key features are racial and ethnic balance, a new student assignment plan, school-based management, and decentralization. The board's current policy on racial/ethnic balance is as stringent as in any district in the country. The goal is to achieve, at each elementary school, a mix among African-American, Hispanic, and "other" students that is "within 5 percentage points of the District average for each of these groups in each of the grade levels." Because all White Plains children attend the same middle school and high school, the issue of racial/ethnic balance is related only to the five elementary schools in the district. White Plains borrowed heavily from the Cambridge plan.

In 1988 White Plains opened its parent information center to help all parents in the district understand the procedures and rules of the choice program. Parents are asked to choose three schools and rank them in order of preference; incoming kindergarteners are guaranteed their school of first choice if they have siblings attending that school. Incoming students are also given preference for their first-choice school if they live in the school's former catchment area. After the guaranteed placements are assigned, a public lottery is held and students are placed on waiting lists which are publicly posted at the center. An average of 89 percent of families receive their first-choice school, and all families who complete the process receive one of their three choices. In 1991, 36 percent of parents with children entering kindergarten chose to send their children to schools outside their former attendance zone. Lorette Young, coordinator of the district's Parent Information Center, has organized an outreach program that includes putting up posters throughout the community in laundromats, bodegas, libraries, health and day-care centers, and churches. These posters include tear-off reminder cards encouraging parents to visit schools. During the first year of the program, 400 visits were scheduled; in 1991, 675 visits were scheduled. Like the parent information center in Fall River, the one in White Plains has become a community center for families and children.

According to Yanofsky and Young, controlled choice has many indirect benefits: school staffs have become more thoughtful and articulate about what they stand for educationally, parents have become more sophisticated about what to look for in schools, the registration process provides an opportunity to make positive contact with the parents of each incoming student, parents have become involved in their children's education, and equal opportunity is made real. In sum, these case studies seem to indicate that controlled choice is a mechanism that provides for educational equity and encourages innovation. Curiously, it has not been controlled choice that has captured the media's attention, nor has the U.S. Department of Education exhibited a strong interest in it. Both the media and the government have been fascinated by market models of educational reform, including privatization and vouchers. Our next case study examines what must surely be one of the most celebrated private-school voucher experiments in the United States. The drama surrounding the voucher movement in Milwaukee is a story worth telling.

The Poor People's Revolt

School vouchers—publicly funded chits or checks that allow families to enroll their children in a private or public school of their choice—have been proposed as a way of reforming education by some policy analysts since at least the late 1950s. If there is one issue that unites the public school establishment, it is vouchers. According to most teachers' unions and other public service organizations, a school voucher program would destroy the public school system because it would remove funds from public schools and allow the best students to opt out of the public system. Still, the idea of vouchers persists. From time to time, liberals such as Christopher Jencks and Theodore Sizer have suggested voucher plans, but in general conservatives have been their strongest advocates. Free-market conservatives are taken with vouchers because they believe in the marketplace as a mechanism for reform and are philosophically committed to public policies that lessen the authority of the state. A key issue is church-state relations; most voucher plans could result in the expenditure of state money in private religious schools.

Ronald Reagan proposed several voucher plans, all of which were eventually defeated in Congress. Superficially, vouchers seem to be the political property of the conservative establishment, which is interested in social profit and the free market and prides itself on understanding the economics of education. Their call is to break the public school monopoly. How ironic, then, that the most celebrated voucher plan in the United States should be the brainchild of an African-American assemblywoman from Milwaukee's North Side. Annette "Polly" Williams is a former welfare mother who earned a degree at the University of Chicago while she raised her four children as a single parent. Representative Williams has worked as a cashier, a clerk, a key-punch operator, and a typist. "I know what it's like to have food stamps and to get that check every month." According to Williams, the real enemies of the poor are not right-wing Republicans but well-meaning liberals who still want to tell black people what to do. "There was a time and a place for their participation, but here we are in the '90s . . . and they still see us as little children who are not able to think and take charge of their lives" (Olson 1990:14–15).

That Williams has become the darling of the voucher movement and of the conservative coalition that supports it is not surprising. After all, if a political supporter of Rev. Jesse Jackson can be for vouchers, will the use of vouchers really lead to increased racial and class stratification? Williams's name has been invoked by high-ranking officials in the U.S. Department of Education, and the Bush administration frequently cited the Milwaukee voucher experiment to show that market models of educational reform can revitalize education in the inner city. It is an interesting political coalition.

When President Bush announced his "G.I. Bill for Children," the educational establishment were markedly absent, but fundamentalist churches were well represented. Fundamentalists support vouchers for the obvious reason that they would like to be able to receive state funds to subsidize their schools. Curiously, another group significantly represented at the event was pro–school-choice inner-city African-Americans. At first glance, this might seem an unlikely combination. What, after all, does a poor inner-city youngster have in common with a fundamentalist minister from suburban Virginia? In my interview with Debra Cruel, formerly of the Landmark Legal Foundation, I discovered the linkage. A leading figure in the conservative African-American political movement, Cruel is also deeply religious, and it was not until she started citing scripture as an ideological justification for school choice that I realized that the link between the African-American conservatives and fundamentalists is religion. Throughout the day I heard that those who were struggling for school choice were doing the Lord's work.

Williams has relentlessly attacked the public school system in Milwaukee, and there is little doubt that she believes in private education; all four of her children were educated in private schools. If we are to believe the *Wall Street Journal*, the voucher plan in Milwaukee represents the best hope for American education. The facts, however, present a somewhat more complicated picture. Milwaukee has educational problems that are typical of big cities. In 1990 only 41 percent of tenth-graders in the public schools tested at or above the national average in math, and only 38 percent of fifth-graders tested at or above the national average in reading. More than half of Milwaukee's nearly ninety-nine thousand public school students are eligible for free lunches because their families live at or below the poverty level, and only 33 percent of Hispanics and 32 percent of African-Americans complete high school. To meet the educational crisis, Milwaukee educators and legislators have introduced magnet schools, and Milwaukee has been court-ordered to integrate its schools through bussing. The policy of bussing is particularly grating to Williams: "We have all our children being bussed all over west hell. You're putting the emphasis on transportation and race, when you need to be talking about education" (Olson 1990:14–15). In 1990 Williams introduced legislation in support of the Milwaukee Parental Choice Law, which allows a thousand low-income Milwaukee students to attend private nonsectarian schools. Their tuition is to be paid for by a $2,500 voucher per student. Funds for the private school vouchers are diverted from the general school funds, which would be otherwise used to support the Milwaukee public schools. The income of families in the choice program cannot be higher than

1.75 times the federal poverty level. For example, a family of four would qualify if its monthly income was at or below $1,853. No more than one percent of the school district's membership may attend private schools under this program in any school year, and no more than 49 percent of a private school's enrollment may consist of pupils attending under the parental choice program. The participating schools must meet four standards:

1. At least 70 percent of the pupils in the program must advance one grade level each year.

2. The average attendance rate for the pupils in the program must be at least 90 percent.

3. At least 80 percent of the pupils in the program must demonstrate "significant academic progress."

4. At least 70 percent of the families of pupils in the program must meet parent-involvement criteria established by the private school.

Fears that wealthy suburban private schools would be the beneficiaries of this legislation have not materialized. The schools participating in the Milwaukee choice program tend to be small and located in the inner city. In fact, the educational question raised by this legislation is whether or not these private schools are actually better than the public schools. Certainly, many newspaper articles have quoted parents and children participating in the program to the effect that they "love choice." In the first year only 341 students participated in the program, and many of them ended up dropping out. One school, the Juanita Virgil Academy, abandoned the program after nonvoucher parents demanded the resumption of religion classes.

Needless to say, the Milwaukee parental choice program has aroused a great deal of public controversy. Wisconsin's superintendent of public instruction, Herbert J. Grover, has been a critic of the voucher plan from its inception. Grover is a supporter of public education and maintains that private-school vouchers will resegregate society and destroy the common school. He calls choice a "gun shot against public schools." Meanwhile, Gov. Tommy Thompson is a strong advocate of choice. After a great deal of litigation, the Wisconsin Supreme Court upheld the constitutionality of the Milwaukee program by a vote of 4 to 3.

Another element of the Milwaukee story bears mentioning. In February 1990, Charles Willie, Michael Alves, and David Hartmann submitted to Robert S. Peterkin, the Milwaukee superintendent of schools, and the Milwaukee Board of School Directors a "Long-Range Educational Equity Plan for Milwaukee Public Schools." Like the controlled-choice plan in Cambridge, the plan submitted by Willie, Alves, and Hartmann promoted choice, guaranteed desegregation, and provided opportunities for improved education. The plan was extremely thorough and incorporated choice-design improvements that were the product of successful controlled-choice experiments in other cities.

The plan, however, was not adopted by the Milwaukee Board of School Directors. There were many reasons for this, the most significant being "yuppy resistance." The blunt fact is that affluent white families are not eager to integrate their children's schools with poor minority children. This reality helps illuminate an observation made to me by Bill Burrow, associate director of President Bush's Office on Competitiveness. He indicated that school choice is popular in the national headquarters of the Republican party but is unpopular among the Republican rank-and-file voters who have moved away from the inner city in part so that their children will not have to attend schools that are racially or socio-economically integrated. With the rejection of the Milwaukee controlled-choice experiment and the national recognition given to Polly Williams's plan, the die may be cast for future voucher programs for inner-city students.

Clearly, it is too early to know whether or not the Milwaukee choice program is educationally effective or, in the final analysis, constitutionally defensible. The significance of the plan, however, goes beyond its immediate consequences; it reflects the uneasy political coalition behind the voucher movement, and it opens the way to the further privatization of American education. Even though the Milwaukee program is limited, it has profound redesign consequences. As I will suggest later, private-school vouchers could lead to a proliferation of market-driven schools whose educational philosophies are questionable, at best.

Unraveling the Complexities of School Choice

Examining, understanding, and critiquing the variety of school choice policies in the United States is a complex process because the phrase "school choice" covers a wide variety of alternative student assignment policies. In Minnesota, school choice means redesigning the way educational services are delivered on a statewide basis; in East Harlem it refers to a district-wide system of magnet schools that allows for some parental and student discretion. Most operational school choice policies fall somewhere between complete redesign of the existing system and minimal change, but the major redesign policies have received the most publicity. School choice is also complex because, unlike building-level reform initiatives, school choice is deeply embedded in the sociological infrastructure of society and the ethos of American education.

The case studies presented above provide some evidence about the range of school choice policies in their social, political, and educational contexts. We have learned that there are a variety of policies and that not all the claims made for school choice are true or at least verifiable. Controlled-choice policies seem to be an effective way of bringing about educational equity and possibly excellence. Last, it is much too early to make a comprehensive assessment about which choice policies have the potential of genuinely revitalizing American education. From a policy perspective, the results of school choice have been uneven.

From a political perspective, though, there is strong evidence that school choice is a meta-reform that deeply touches certain fundamental issues in American life. Rightly or wrongly, many Americans see public education as having failed. In this sense, school choice grew out of our anxiety concerning our economic competitiveness. By some mysterious process, school choice will make us "number one." This leads us to wonder, what is the actual relationship between school choice and student achievement? What are the outcomes of school choice? Do parental involvement and school choice affect how educational services are actually delivered? My experience and research have shown me that there is far less parental involvement in the private sector than some recent research has indicated. In fact, a mythology has grown up around private schools that under different circumstances would be banal. Under the present conditions, however, this mythology represents an ideological distortion of the real world of education and, as such, may represent a threat to genuine reform. In the next chapter we ask fundamental questions: Does choice make a difference? And if so, in what ways?

4. Does Choice Make a Difference?

Research results are often the subject of intense partisan debate. Intellectual positions are won or lost and reputations made or unmade. Compared to the school choice controversy, however, most research squabbles seem petty. School choice data are grasped by proponents and opponents as intellectual weapons to be used in the struggle for symbolic and material dominance. The results of school choice studies are front-page news.

As an example of how rough-and-tumble the politics of school choice research can be, consider the recent publication of the Carnegie Foundation's study of school choice. The study's most important findings include the following: "Seventy percent of parents with children in public school do not favor sending them to another public or private school; in states where school choice has been adopted, less than 2 percent of parents participate in the program; and parents who transfer their children to another school do so mostly for nonacademic reasons" (1992:20). The report includes an essay by Ernest L. Boyer, president of the foundation. "School Choice in Perspective" is a reasoned but impassioned argument for supporting neighborhood public schools. Boyer is skeptical about the power of choice to transform education, but he does acknowledge that "choice, at its best, empowers parents, stimulates teachers to be more creative and, most important, gives students a new sense of attachment to their schools and to learning" (1992:1). His remarks provoked an almost immediate response from leading choice advocates. Chester E. Finn, Jr., suggested that the report exhibited "a kind of backlash, or nip-in-the-bud stance, toward choice and toward privatization." Terry M. Moe, whose work I will discuss later in this chapter, referred to the report as "a real smear job." He continued, "I think it's grossly unfair and basically an effort to forward their own agenda." And Joe Nathan claimed that he found "64 significant misstatements of fact or distortions in one chapter" (Olson 1992).

Cutting through this rhetoric is the task of this chapter. I have collected all the information I could about the outcomes of school choice and evaluated the soundness of the research approaches and the credibility of the results. Four questions have guided my thinking: (1) What is the relationship between school choice and student achievement? (2) What is the relationship between school choice and other school outcomes? (3) What is the relationship between school choice and equity? (4) What is the relationship between school choice and community?

Unpacking the Research Problem

The rift between educational research and practice is notoriously wide (Cookson 1987a). Many researchers have attempted to bridge this gap and have developed astute and meaningful methodologies to bring research closer to the real world of teachers and students. Yet, without disparaging these efforts in any way, the fact remains that evaluating educational change and reform eventually raises measurement issues that are closely related to conceptual issues. Many people writing about school choice have simplistic notions of what constitutes empirical proof, or even what constitutes logical reasoning. Researchers often assume cause and effect. In its simplest expression, this thinking takes the form of a research model that begins with student inputs and examines student outcomes as they are influenced by the characteristics of schools. This model is useful as a way of organizing data, but it can also create illusions of symmetry. Schools do not operate apart from the social context. Cause and effect are not always so easy to disentangle. For instance, schools with high-status student bodies are more likely to be judged effective than schools with lower-status students, regardless of the schools' organizational characteristics. As a consequence, high-status families will be drawn to schools that already include a critical mass of high-status students. In this sense, inputs and outputs influence each other. A one-directional model of causation poorly reflects the interactions between school and society.

What do we mean by student achievement anyway? What factors contribute to it and how can they be measured? Unfortunately, the social sciences have only the grossest measures of these very delicate phenomena. Does the Stanford-Binet test really capture intelligence? Simplistic measures of complex human behaviors can bring a pseudo-order to what is in fact a very messy real-life situation. Moreover, Americans tend to put undue faith in numbers. Researchers who have the numbers are believed to be knowledgeable, but, as we shall see, numbers do not speak for themselves, nor do they always speak the truth. The human mind behind the numbers guides them and in doing so may help us understand social relationships or may provide a statistical smoke screen behind which to hide them. Statistical interpretation is difficult, complex, and problematic. This observation has been repeated so often it has achieved the status of a cliché. But—and this is significant—the school choice coalition is far from being yet another academic camp. It is a powerful, nationally sponsored political movement that has an explicit agenda for reshaping American education and, in the process, reshaping American society. Statistics in the service of power are social weapons.

Because the chain of causation is so complex, interactive, and difficult to trace, serious scholarship has found few, if any, measurable relationships between school governance and student achievement. According to Clune

(1990:394), "Direct evidence of a positive effect of governance on achievement is scarce, partly because of a dearth of governance structures to study, and partly because of a lack of adequate research." If, for the sake of argument, however, we were to grant that the chain of causation could be identified, there would still be serious measurement and interpretation problems. The fundamental issue is one of statistical control. To what degree has the researcher drawn an accurate statistical and social map? If the map is too simple, then observed relationships may be spurious because the researcher has overlooked an important alternative explanation of the findings. For example, research has repeatedly shown that student family background is highly related to student outcomes regardless of the characteristics of the schools students attend. A "good" school may, therefore, be the result of a "good" student body. Some families, for instance, have more of a "taste for education" than others. How do we measure this proclivity? Simple measures of socio-economic status are inadequate, even as proxy measures, because they are based only on family income, education, and occupation. The socio-psychological dynamics that drive some families to forgo material benefits for the sake of their children's education are far too subtle to be captured by such gross measures. In sum, the attempt to establish a statistical relationship between school governance and student achievement presents a thicket of measurement issues that often render apparent relationships spurious. A statistically significant finding may be substantively trivial and may seduce the researcher into believing that congruent findings are consequential.

Types of Choice Research

Essentially, there are four types of choice research: controlled experimental design, comparisons of public and private schools, qualitative studies of public school choice, and program evaluations. None of these literatures is very strong, although there is now a great deal of data comparing public and private schools. We will examine the public/private school literature in some depth and make reference to a select number of program evaluations. Below, we will briefly touch on the controlled experimental design research and on the qualitative studies of public schools of choice, generally referred to as magnet schools.

The earliest systematic attempt to evaluate school choice occurred in the Alum Rock, California, School District, near San José. This experiment was funded by the federal government as a way of determining the educational and social effects a voucher plan would have on a school system. In some ways, the Alum Rock voucher experiment reflected the liberal egalitarian social policies advocated by Christopher Jencks, author and coauthor of many important studies, the most famous of which is *Inequality* (1972). Originally, the Alum Rock experiment was to last five years and be a test case for vouchers; only the public schools of the district participated. Prof. Patricia Lines, who participated in the experiment, believed then and still believes that vouchers are a way of helping the disadvantaged, but she told me that the politics involved in implementing a voucher system in Alum Rock were so intense that its designers feared it would never be accepted by the teachers of the school district if private schools were included.

At the peak of the experiment in 1974–1975, fourteen participating schools offered fifteen mini-programs. The Rand Corporation conducted a five-year evaluation of the experiment, but the results are inconclusive (Capell 1978). To begin with, test-score data for the students in regular schools were unavailable for the first two years of the study. More important, the experiment changed dramatically in nature during the last year. Only two years were available for analysis, and only the reading scores were usable. Nevertheless, the results of the survey are interesting. When, for instance, parents were asked to choose between "traditional classrooms" and "open classrooms," the overwhelming majority selected the traditional ones, although affluent parents were more likely to select the open-classroom option than other parents (Bridge and Blackman 1978). On the basis of this study, it appears that most parents at the outset of the experiment preferred their neighborhood schools. But as families gained experience, they began to choose more distant schools. There was no indication that students' reading scores improved as a result of school choice. A key question in the Alum Rock experiment was whether choice would "upset" racial balance and thus lead to greater segregation. Overall, racial balance remained fairly stable. There was an increased desire among Hispanics for bilingual education. It is not surprising, therefore, that bilingual classes enrolled a disproportionately high number of Hispanic students.

The Rand report on the experiment did reveal, however, that "socially advantaged families" were better informed about school choice options. Moreover, advantaged families tended to learn about the choice program from written material, while socially disadvantaged parents were more likely to obtain information by word of mouth. Over time, many of these differences diminished. Equal access to information is critical if school choice is not to lead to greater racial and class segregation among students (Elmore 1986). In Alum Rock it appeared that over time there was equality of information among families, whatever their income level or ethnicity. The Alum Rock experiment offers no conclusive evidence about the effects of school choice on student achievement or racial balance in part because the experiment was politically compromised, but also in part because the relationship between governance and achievement is extremely difficult to document.

The same problem arises in qualitative studies of public school choice. In her book *Different by Design* (1986), Prof. Mary Hayward Metz called attention to the possibilities and problems inherent in creating magnet schools. In essence, a magnet school is one that is given extra resources and develops a specific mission in order to attract students who would not ordinarily attend that school. The creation of magnet schools was part of a general effort in the 1970s to promote peaceful racial integration and to create innovative schools. Metz's work indicates that magnet schools can have desirable effects on parental involvement, faculty morale, and some student outcomes. But much depends upon how the magnet plan is designed and on how the community and school unite in the implementation phase. Rolf K. Blank (1989) reported that among the magnet schools he studied, the best performance was achieved by those that had strong central office support, energetic and able leaders and teaching staffs, and well-planned programs.

These results are not surprising. Most effective schools share these characteristics. In a study of effective schools, Caroline H. Persell and I found that they generally have effective principals. In fact, the most important element in creating an effective school is a dynamic, competent, and committed leadership team (Persell and Cookson 1982). Magnet school programs throughout the country have aroused a great deal of controversy. Activists such as Polly Williams find magnet schools particularly exasperating because while white children are being bussed into the inner city to attend a magnet school, African-American children are being bussed all over Milwaukee to attend neighborhood schools of no particular academic stature. The magnet school is a two-edged educational sword; it helps a few students but has little or no impact on the educational system as a whole. Because of the nature of the research on magnet schools, we have little idea of their impact on student achievement or on educational redesign. We turn now to those studies which bear directly on the claim that school choice is related to student achievement.

Achievement by Association

In this section we will examine the research of several authors who make similar claims concerning the relationship between school choice and student achievement. These studies are considered together because they suffer from the same flaw: they identify a correlation and call it causation. Specifically, we will examine the findings of Nancy Paulu and her colleagues, who guided the proceedings at the 1989 White House Workshop on Choice in Education. Then we will turn to the work of Seymour Fliegel and Raymond J. Domanico, both of whom have made strong claims that choice policies in Manhattan's Community School District 4 in East Harlem have led to substantial achievement gains for students in that district. My colleague Diane Harrington and I have written elsewhere that these authors confuse cause with consequence and have unduly magnified the importance of choice as an instrument of school improvement (Harrington and Cookson 1992).

In *Improving Schools and Empowering Parents: Choice in American Education* (1989), Paulu claims that choice policies lead to higher reading and math scores, lower rates of school violence, and higher attendance rates. Paulu's approach to data collection is eclectic, to say the least. She simply finds measures of association in her review of the literature and interprets them as being related causally. To cite one concrete example, on the basis of an interview with Deputy Superintendent Juana Dainis in District 4, Paulu reports that in 1972 the district ranked last in reading scores among New York City's thirty-two community school districts, and that by 1988 it had risen to between twentieth and sixteenth place, with 84 percent of the East Harlem eighth-graders judged competent writers. But Paulu's research strategy is based on what amounts to hearsay, makes no attempt to account for other possible explanations, does not clearly define achievement measures, and interprets alleged associations causally, leading the unsophisticated consumer of educational research to the erroneous conclusion that there is a direct link between choice and achievement.

Seymour Fliegel is a member of the board of the Manhattan Institute. In an article entitled "Creative Non-Compliance" he claims that 15.9 percent of the students in grades two through nine were reading at or above their expected level in 1973, and that 64.9 percent were reading at or above their expected level by 1988. He attributes this astonishing rise to the "introduction of parental choice" (1990:15). If this is correct, we would expect to find similar results in similar studies, but we do not. In a study conducted after the Alum Rock experiment, no evidence was found that open enrollment affects students' reading achievement, perceptions of themselves, or social skills (Capell 1978). Fliegel's data on the percentage of students at or above grade level in mathematics are also limited. He reports that between 1982 and 1985, the percentage of students at or above grade level in mathematics in District 4 rose from 41.8 to 49 to 50.6 to 51. These data tell us virtually nothing about the relationship between governance and student achievement.

Raymond J. Domanico, also of the Manhattan Institute, likewise claims that school choice improves student achievement. Not surprisingly, his data are almost identical to Fliegel's and suffer from the same problems. Domanico does attempt to expand on these data somewhat by comparing District 4 reading scores to citywide reading scores. But the data make little sense because to compare District 4 to all the districts in the city masks variation and oversimplifies dramatically. To take an example from Domanico's data, it appears that the percentage of students citywide who were reading at their expected level rose from 33.8 percent in 1974 to 65 percent in 1988. In the same period, the percentage of students in District 4 who were reading at or above their expected level rose from 15.3 to 62.5. Two immediate observations arise from these reported results: Much of the rise in reading scores in District 4 can be accounted for by the rise in scores citywide; and it is very difficult to isolate school choice as a causal factor in elevating reading scores when scores also rise dramatically in community school districts that do not have school choice policies. Moreover, one has to wonder if the literacy rate among elementary school students really rose so dramatically in fourteen years. Let us not forget that school districts have a vested interest in reporting higher reading scores. One simple question we might ask is, Do all the students from all the districts take the test?

Interestingly, Domanico's own data indicate that math achievement levels in District 4 actually declined between 1983 and 1988. While this decline is not dramatic, it certainly calls into question the author's assertion that students in District 4 are "doing mathematics better than they did 15 years ago and better than their peers in most New York City districts" (1989:24). Both Fliegel and Domanico also make a number of claims about the rates at which students from District 4 are admitted to selective New York City public schools and to private schools nationally. These data are unreliable because the factors related to private school admission are far too complex to be summarized by simply listing the schools that admit District 4 students (see Cookson and Persell 1985 for a discussion of private school admission practices).

Does the inadequacy of these data analyses mean that school choice is unrelated to student achievement? No. It simply means that the evidence presented by these particular authors is unconvincing and, in the long run, undermines their own position because it exposes their claims to methodological criticisms that are seemingly unanswered, even unacknowledged. There are other studies, however, that use very sophisticated methodologies to make their case. In the next section we will analyze the claims of some private-school researchers who have joined in the school choice debate by claiming that private schools "do it better" and should therefore serve as models for public schools. What evidence is there that private schools are more educationally productive than public schools?

The Private School "Effect"

When *High School Achievement: Public, Catholic, and Private Schools Compared* was published in 1982, it caused a great deal of controversy. The authors, James Coleman, Thomas Hoffer, and Sally Kilgore, claimed that when they compared the average test scores of public and private school sophomores and seniors, there was not one subject in which public school students scored higher. In reading, vocabulary, mathematics, science, civics, and writing tests, private school students outperformed public school students, sometimes by a wide margin. For example, the test included thirty-three mathematics questions. On average, public school sophomores answered eighteen questions correctly, Catholic and other private school sophomores on average answered twenty-two correctly, and elite private school sophomores averaged thirty correct answers. Seniors' test scores followed the same pattern.

Are these differences between sectors due to student selection, or do schools also affect cognitive skills? After conducting a series of regression analyses, Coleman, Hoffer, and Kilgore concluded (1982:177): "In the examination of effects on achievement, statistical controls on family background are introduced, in order to control on those background characteristics that are most related to achievement. The achievement differences between the private sectors and public sector are reduced (more for other private schools than for Catholic schools) but differences remain." In other words, there *is* a private school effect on student achievement.

The results reported by Coleman and his colleagues have been criticized sharply (Alexander and Pallas 1983; Goldberger and Cain 1982). The essential issue is whether these results are substantial enough to support the argument that private schools, particularly Catholic schools, are superior learning environments when compared to public schools. For instance, when we examine the Coleman, Hoffer, and Kilgore data in terms of student cognitive growth between the sophomore and senior years for the three types of schools analyzed, we discover that the percentage differences among the three sectors are relatively insignificant when compared with the cognitive growth for all students in that cohort. That is, even if there is some private school effect, it is unlikely that it is significant enough from an educational point of view to justify the claim that private schools are markedly superior to public schools.

Jencks (1985:133), in a reanalysis of the Coleman, Hoffer, and Kilgore data, concluded: "Public school students' scores on the 'High School and Beyond' tests rise by an average of .15 standard deviations per year. Catholic-school students' scores rise by an average of .18 standard deviations per year if they start at the Catholic-school mean and by .19 standard deviations per year if they start at the public-school mean. The annual increment attributable to Catholic schooling thus averages .03 or .04 standard deviations per year. By conventional standards this is a tiny effect, hardly worth study. But conventional standards may be misleading in this case."

Jencks reports that in the final analysis the vaunted "Catholic school effect" is quite small and probably insignificant in terms of student learning. He recognizes, however, that Coleman's findings have important political ramifications because they appear to validate the academic superiority of private schools, which in turn may promote policies that result in public funding of private schools. Alexander and Pallas also found that the Catholic school effect was quite small—even tiny—in substantive terms. They conclude (1985:122): "What then of Coleman, Hoffer, and Kilgore's claim that Catholic schools are educationally superior to public schools? If trivial advantage is what they mean by such a claim, then we suppose we would have to agree. But judged against reasonable benchmarks, there is little basis for this conclusion."

Other researchers who have reanalyzed the Coleman, Hoffer, and Kilgore data for evidence of a private school effect have also found almost nothing. For instance, Lee and Bryk (1989) concluded that, after accounting for individual student differences, variations in achievement gains were the result of racial and socio-economic school composition, average number of advanced courses taken, amount of homework assigned, and staff problems in the school. Whether a school was private was virtually insignificant. One can use the Coleman, Hoffer, and Kilgore data to argue for or against choice. If private schools truly are better than public schools, we could predict that a choice system which included both public and private schools could lead to further social stratification among the consumers of education (Elmore 1990; Cookson 1991a). On the other hand—and this is the argument made by Coleman and his colleagues—private schools can serve as models for public schools and for this reason should be included in choice plans (Coleman and Hoffer 1987; Coleman 1992).

The Milwaukee school choice experiment provides a small but significant case study as to whether the inclusion of private schools in choice programs leads to higher academic achievement. The political scientist John Witte, in his study of achievement in the first year of the Milwaukee plan, found: "As a group, the choice students went up somewhat in reading, but declined in math. They moved ahead of the low-income comparison group in reading, but remained behind in math" (1992:21–22). None of these results was statistically significant. Clearly, it is much too early to make definitive remarks about the effects of the voucher program on student achievement in Milwaukee. I would expect, however, that vouchers will have little effect on student achievement. Attendance at a private school by no means guarantees greater measurable learning.

As someone who has worked in private schools and studied them (Cookson and Persell 1985; Persell and Cookson 1985; Cookson 1989), I am unconvinced that Coleman and his colleagues have been able to deal adequately with the problem of selectivity bias. Private schools attract families who are wealthier than average (Cookson 1989:62–63), are usually quite knowledgeable about their educational options, and have faith in the power of education in the intellectual and status marketplace. Elmore, who has examined some of the effects of choice in relation to education and health care, concludes (1990:313–14): "It seems unlikely that policies designed to give clients greater choice in highly complex, inscrutable structures will result in anything other than a reshuffling of opportunities in favor of those who are willing to incur the costs of information-seeking. It also seems unlikely that making greater choice available to clients, without increasing opportunities for clients to engage and interrogate institutions, will do anything other than increase the random movement of clients among providers."

In other words, families and individuals who are able and willing to investigate their options when choosing schools or health-care facilities maintain an advantage over those who are less able or inclined to investigate the choices available to them. Returning to the discussion of the complex nature of the chain of causation, we can see that there is an interaction between family preference and student performance when we compare public and private schools. Therefore, simple intersectional comparisons produce results that obscure the complex relationship between schools and a highly stratified society. If there is a private school effect, should it be the basis for a policy that might well result in further academic and social stratification? Moreover, does the relatively small size of this effect justify the reorganization of the American elementary and secondary school system?

The dialogue concerning the relative merits of public and private schools has been taken beyond the findings of Coleman and his colleagues. John E. Chubb and Terry M. Moe, in *Politics, Markets, and America's Schools* (1990), have argued that, without the deregulation of the American public school system, there is little hope for genuine reform. In the next section, we will examine their evidence that market-driven schools lead to higher student achievement.

Markets and High Marks: Is There a Relationship?

Chubb and Moe argue that they have convincing data that market-driven schools are superior to democratically controlled schools in producing higher cognitive outcomes among students. Of the authors examined thus far, Chubb and Moe make the strongest claims. Their analyses are extremely complex. Their measure of student achievement is five of the six standardized tests that were administered as part of the Coleman, Hoffer, and Kilgore survey. These paper-and-pencil tests were given to a cohort of sophomores in the spring of 1980 and retaken by the same students at the end of their senior year in 1982. Chubb and Moe then created an index of achievement based on the differences between sophomore and senior scores. That is, they calculated the gains students registered between their sophomore and senior years on each test and then aggregated these gains into an index. On the basis of this technique, they make the following claim (1990:71): "Gain scores measure only the learning that takes place during high school whereas scores for the sophomore and senior years alone are contaminated by many years of prior learning. Since our main purpose is to account for the effectiveness of high schools in promoting student achievement, it is especially important to factor out of the analysis those influences—school, family, peer groups—that precede the high school years."

This statement suffers from serious errors of logic. First, family background does not cease to operate between the tenth and twelfth grades. One cannot claim that measuring differences between scores somehow removes all other confounding variables. Second, the authors admit that for many students, the achievement gains made between their sophomore and senior years were minimal. According to Chubb and Moe, the gain scores indicate that students learned only a fraction of what they might have learned between their sophomore and senior years. The methodological conclusion should be that gain scores are probably inadequate in attempting to capture the actual variability related to cognitive growth. To compound the problem, the authors divide their sample of schools into quartiles and compare the lowest-quartile schools with the highest-quartile schools across a number of variables. Thus they ignore the variation in the middle of the continuum, which essentially diminishes the total variation within their sample. Not surprisingly, most of the schools in the highest quartile are market-driven (that is, private).

Chubb and Moe next proceed to interpret student achievement gains in terms of grade equivalents. This is a slippery technique because it magnifies their results. In effect, the authors are equating achievement gains with specific time units. Suppose, for the sake of argument, I were to say that one unit of achievement gain was equivalent to three months of schooling. I would then be able to claim that three units of achievement gain were equivalent to a full year of schooling. Does this sound a little strained? But according to Chubb and Moe (1990:140): "All things being equal, a student in an effectively organized school should achieve at least a half year more than a student in an ineffectively organized school over the last two years of high school. If that difference can be extrapolated to the normal high school experience, an effectively organized school may increase the achievement of its students by more than one full year. That is a substantial effect indeed." This would indeed be a substantial effect, if it were true. My hunch is that the authors have so magnified their results by altering the unit of analysis from a score to a time frame that they have lost sight of their own finding, which indicates that there are very few achievement gains between the sophomore and senior years of high school.

The heart of the Chubb and Moe analysis as it relates to student achievement is in chapter 4 of their book. After a great deal of preliminary discussion, the authors present us with a model of student achievement. The dependent variable in this model is the total gain in student achievement. The independent variables include students' academic ability and family background, the background of the student body, the school's resources and organization, and what the authors call "selection bias correction." To determine the separate effects of these variables on student achievement, the authors estimated a series of linear regression models. The coefficients of a regression model provide estimates of the effects of each explanatory variable on the dependent variable when the other explanatory variables are held constant.

The Chubb and Moe model suffers from several problems. To begin with, their key variable, which they call school organization, is so comprehensive as to be incomprehensible. The variable includes the following measures (1990:124): "graduation requirements; priority of academic excellence; principal's motivation; principal's teaching esteem (principal's dedication to teaching, estimated excellence of teachers); teacher professionalism (teacher influence, efficacy, absenteeism); staff harmony (teacher collegiality, teacher cooperation, principal's vision); percentage of students in academic track; homework assignments; classroom administrative routines; disciplinary fairness and effectiveness." Thus the key variable in Chubb and Moe's analysis, school organization, is an omnibus measure so general in nature that it is impossible to tell what it purports to measure. Finally, all this quantification is drawn together in table 4.8, "Estimates of

Models of Student Achievement Gains Using Comprehensive Measure of School Organization." It turns out that the authors' model explains only 5 percent of the variance in achievement. Given that their sample size is well over seven thousand students, the model explains remarkably little of the variation. I submit that any model that leaves 95 percent of the variation unexplained is of extremely limited value.

It is reasonable to ask whether Chubb and Moe have created a very elaborate analytic superstructure on a very small and shaky statistical foundation. Based on their own analyses, they do not know what the causes of student achievement are, and they certainly do not know if their results can be attributed to differences in school governance. To bridge this gulf, they spend a great deal of time discussing effective and ineffective schools and the virtues of private schools. I think it fair to say that Chubb and Moe's argument that student achievement is directly linked to school organization must be taken with an analytic grain of salt.

In a recent study entitled "Choice in Education: Some Effects," Stephen Plank, Kathryn Schiller, Barbara Schneider, and James Coleman (1992) found that in terms of eighth-grade achievement, students who attended choice schools did not do as well as private school students or students who were assigned to neighborhood schools. Choice students did do better than students who attended magnet schools or vocational-technical schools. If we compare the achievement scores of students in the tenth grade with those of eighth-graders, we see that choice students do not make dramatic gains when compared to students in other types of schools. The authors examined the proportion of eighth-graders and tenth-graders who planned to attend college. They found (1992:10) that 65 percent of choice students, 85 percent of private school students, and 68 percent of students attending magnet schools were planning to attend a four-year college. What these data indicate is that choice schools do not have the dramatic effect on achievement that its advocates have claimed. Certainly, the recent Carnegie Foundation report (1992) on school choice calls into question the hypothesized positive relationship between school choice and student achievement.

Establishing a positive relationship between school governance and student achievement has proved extremely difficult because the structure of most schools isolates the technical core of teaching and learning from the policies emanating from administrators' offices. There is, however, more to a school than student achievement scores. Schools are communities, living human organizations that develop personalities of their own. Some school cultures are more conducive to student learning and a sense of well-being than other cultures. It may be that school choice is weakly related to student achievement but strongly related to school culture and, therefore, indirectly related to students' academic and personal growth. Our fixation with numbers sometimes blinds us to the larger lived experience. In the next section we examine the evidence concerning the relationship between school choice and school improvement.

Choice and the Creation of School Communities

What makes a school good? Schools are not only sites for learning, they are also sites for living. When a hundred or more children or young people and adults unite to create a learning environment, a dynamic is created. If the dynamic is positive, the school can be an oasis; if it is negative, the school can feel like a jail. The fact that schools create strong cultures is overlooked by too many policymakers. These cultures affect the living experiences of children. We know very little about how school choice influences school culture directly. We do know anecdotally that the process of creating choice can generate a sense of renewal that is worthwhile in itself. Some of the following discussion is based on informed speculation, yet it is important that efforts be made to draw plausible connections between school choice and the creation of school communities.

The educator Mary Driscoll (1992:11), in her study of parent and student beliefs about public schools of choice, found that, on average, parents in choice schools were more satisfied with their children's education.

They believe more strongly that their child enjoyed school and was challenged by it; that the homework assigned was worthwhile and that the school was a safe place. They spent more time talking to their child about high school plans and were contacted less frequently about their child's behavior. Surprisingly, they did not exhibit higher expectations for their child's education in terms of level of completion (B.A., Ph.D., and so on). In other words, although they had significantly positive beliefs about their child's school experience, they did not translate these beliefs into higher expectations for completion of college or professional degrees.

Driscoll also found that while students who attended schools of choice did not have higher test scores than other students, they "clearly believed that their experiences with teachers were better than did the students in the matched schools." As Driscoll points out, there is a paradox here: whether or not they change minds, choice schools may change the "hearts" of students and parents. Driscoll offers several explanations of why this may be the case, but perhaps the most compelling is that choice parents believe that the school their child is attending is better because it is selective. That is, the very act of choosing creates an aura of specialness.

My research confirms Driscoll's findings. Schools of choice may not be objectively better than other schools, but there is a sense of being special. I have already mentioned the rural magnet school in Miltona, Minnesota. The very fact that families chose this school provides them with a sense of ownership. The sociologist John Meyer discussed the "chartering effect" in education more than twenty years ago. According to Meyer (1972:111), "A charter is an institutionalized agreement that a given program, college, or system of colleges is to produce and does produce a given kind of person." In our work in private schools, Caroline H. Persell and I have used Meyer's concept of charter to explain the attraction of private schools for certain parents and the power of private schools to lift their graduates into selective colleges (Persell and Cookson 1985; Cookson and Persell 1985). Choice schools can appear to be selective and thus adopt some of the cultural characteristics of academically and socially "superior" schools. In our examination of private schools we learned that a school's external authority or charter may have little relationship to the quality of education it provides. Driscoll continues, "It is possible, then, that selective or choice schools establish a charter that seems to promise greater access to superior academic opportunities. Meyer's theory would suggest that this special sense of mission in the school is transmitted to students and parents (perhaps through the selection process) and is reflected in their relatively greater 'investment' in academic values (i.e., agreement with the statement 'the homework assigned is worthwhile')." Driscoll concludes, "There is little evidence in this data that making schools more selective makes them better, if we use academic achievement as our criteria for evaluation. . . . Merely improving choice in education will not serve as a panacea for improving school performance" (1992:15,22).

To Joe Nathan these are fighting words. He is convinced that school choice directly improves the lives of students and the academic climates of schools. In his examination of the effects of school choice in Minnesota, he found (1991:144) that choice was responsible for:

- dramatic increases in aspiration levels among students who were not doing well. Percentages of students who said they planned to graduate from high school and to enter college or vocational training increased from 19.4 to 39.5 percent in one program, from 21.6 to 42.9 percent in another, and from 6.2 to 41.2 percent in the third.

- a significant number of dropouts returning to school. More than one-third of the participants in the Second Chance Program were dropouts.

- significant increases in student satisfaction with school, rising from about 25 to 75 percent.

- major increases in the number of students reporting success in school. More than 80 percent said they were more successful in their choice school or program than in their former school.

Nathan cites the work of Prof. Mary Anne Raywid, who concluded in 1989 that providing choice among public schools helped increase student achievement and graduation rates. Moreover, when teachers are given a chance to establish new schools, they have higher morale. Evidence from District 4 in East Harlem does support Nathan's contention that when teachers are given the opportunity to establish new schools, a veritable burst of creativity seems to result (Harrington and Cookson 1992). Most individuals who enter the teaching profession are idealistic, and some are visionary. Educational choice offers them an opportunity to express their creativity that they would not have if there were no school choice. Moreover, many of the benefits of school choice are indirect in that choice policies build school communities and cultures that cannot be measured quantitatively. In Cambridge, Fall River, and White Plains, we have seen that choice leads to school improvement because it compels parents to become involved in the lives of the schools to which they send their children. Certainly, the establishment of parent information centers is itself a significant school improvement, whether or not the existence of these centers leads directly to higher student achievement. Ownership is a key ingredient in building a school community, and as the work of Driscoll and others has shown, choice is a method of creating a sense of educational ownership among families and of binding families closer to the schools their children attend.

School Choice and Life Arithmetic

Critics of school choice have often claimed that choice policies are little more than "new improved sorting machines" (Moore and Davenport 1990). They argue that choice schools will cream off the best students and that the resulting system will only intensify racial and class segregation. Proponents of choice argue the opposite: that choice will give poor people the same educational opportunities as wealthy people. Certainly, one of the primary functions of American education is to provide young people with equal educational opportunities so that their life chances are not foreshortened on account of their parents' race, class, or ethnicity. From its inception, public education was meant to be the great equalizer. I think it fair to say that in recent years the public school system has essentially failed in this mission. The life arithmetic of the overwhelming majority of children is that their social-class destination will be identical, or very similar, to their social-class origin. This is a reality of American education and American life.

Will school choice restratify the educational system and further distance minorities from the rest of the population? Will choice separate the rich from the poor, native-language speakers from non-native-language speakers? How will choice affect the life arithmetic of young Americans who are learning-disabled, emotionally disturbed, or just different? Would a full-blown choice plan lead to thousands of designer schools that lack public accountability in terms of promoting basic democratic values? Many advocates of choice challenge the value of the common school, even promoting private schools as the new common schools. But what evidence do we have that freedom of choice leads to equality of opportunity? These are fundamental questions about the effects of school choice on the life arithmetic of students.

In understanding the relationship between school choice and equity, it is critical to ask not only who supports choice but who actually takes advantage of school choices when they have them. If, for instance, middle-class and upper-middle-class white students are more active choosers than minority students, then in all likelihood choice will have a pronounced "creaming effect." If, on the other hand, minority students are active choosers, then fears of resegregation may be exaggerated. The evidence we have concerning students' patterns of choice is extremely limited. We have already seen, for instance, that in Minnesota only a tiny percentage of children choose to attend schools outside their district. The early evidence from the Alum Rock study seems to indicate that more educated parents are more likely to engage in the process of choosing their children's schools than are parents with less education. One of the questions that has haunted the school choice movement is whether or not poor parents are educated or motivated enough to participate meaningfully in the choice process. Social-scientific research has shown a positive relationship between information levels and social class on such topics as child-rearing practices, nutrition, and general information (Bauch 1989:286). Interestingly, the Alum Rock study found that over time poor parents became as knowledgeable as affluent parents, although the latter relied more on printed material. Patricia Bauch (301–02) examined how poor parents choose Catholic schools and concluded, "Despite what some would fear, it is not that poor parents are not able to practice consumer choice behavior. Rather, poor parents take longer to acquire information; over time they catch up and become aware at the same level as non-poor parents." Bauch believes that poor and minority parents need more time and more diverse opportunities to acquire sophisticated consumer strategies.

In a recent study, Coleman, Schiller, and Schneider compared responses to choice among a national sample of African-Americans, Hispanics, Asian-Americans, and Anglos. They also compared the predicted responses of parents at three educational levels: those who completed high school only, those who had some education beyond high school, and those who had a four-year college degree or more. They found that "minority or immigrant status appears to bring a special responsiveness to opportunity for choice in education that is not apparent among whites of comparable backgrounds. Students from African-American and Hispanic backgrounds, although quite disadvantaged in terms of income and parents' education, showed response to opportunities for choice in the public sector and in the religious private sector, and are making educational investments outside of school that are quite beyond the average for their income levels." On the other hand, the authors found that "the least well-educated parents (the greatest majority of whom are native whites) show the lowest responsiveness to almost every form of opportunity for choice or investment in their children's education" (1991:42). Simplifying somewhat, we may say that a well-educated African-American family is more likely to exercise school choice than a poorly educated white family.

Great Britain has been experimenting with school choice for some time. J. Douglas Willms and Frank H. Echols examined the background of the families that were most likely to participate actively in choosing schools for their children. Their findings (1992:i) show that parents who exercised choice were "more highly educated and had more prestigious occupations than those who sent their child to the designated school. Choosers tended to select schools with higher mean socioeconomic status and higher mean levels of attainment. However, the chosen schools did not differ substantially from designated schools in their students' attainment, once account had been taken of the background characteristics of pupils entering them. The results suggest that the choice process is increasing between-school segregation, which may produce greater inequalities in attainment between social class groups." In other words, at least in the initial stages of an unregulated school choice plan, there may be a significant creaming effect. The consequence may be to impoverish schools intellectually in working-class neighborhoods and to enrich schools in middle-class neighborhoods. These findings are sobering.

One way to mitigate the effects of creaming is to assign students to schools by lottery. The sociologist Robert Crain studied New York City magnet schools to determine if it is "possible" to construct a market that does not produce inequality. New York is famous for such magnet schools as Stuyvesant High School, the Bronx High School of Science, and the LaGuardia High School for the Performing Arts. New York eighth-graders indicate the high school they would like to attend. Career magnet schools are allowed to select 50 percent of their students; the other half are assigned randomly. Specifically, the city has mandated random selection for all magnet programs that prepare students for careers in business, law, health practice, applied science, and applied humanities. When Crain examined the impact of the lottery on schools, he noted first that magnet schools seemed to be pushed by student demand to offer career training. He also found that fears that eighth-graders might make childish choices were not supported by the data and that career magnet programs were related to the development of innovative instructional strategies and increased faculty morale. He found little evidence that randomly selected students were treated differently than other students. In sum, Crain's research indicates that a lottery system can produce a system of choice that is relatively equitable. He acknowledges, however, that "even in New York, there are important forces pushing the system toward inequity" (1992:1).

My own observations about who selects choice schools conform to the data cited above. Fewer people exercise the option to choose schools than choice advocates are willing to acknowledge. Educated parents are more likely to take advantage of choice than less-educated parents. Minority families are more likely to exercise choice than white families. Access to information is critical if choice is not to produce an increasingly stratified school system. It seems evident to me that the alternative-schools model of choice does run the risk of stratifying schools and students because there are no mechanisms to ensure that creaming will not occur. There is early evidence that restratification is already taking place in those states that allow unrestricted interdistrict choice (Wilkerson 1992). Controlled choice, on the other hand, is quite likely to bring about equitable results in terms of the racial backgrounds of students who attend choice schools.

Certainly, a key issue in considering the relationship between school choice and equity is whether choice schools create selective environments that partially privatize them. As we have noted, the distinction between private and public education has become increasingly blurred, and with the creation of charter schools this tendency will continue. Nonetheless, there are important equity considerations if choice schools develop different demographic profiles than nonchoice schools. In a study entitled "Educational Choice: The Stratifying Effects of Selecting Schools and Courses," Valerie Lee found that "all reforms must be scrutinized in regard to their effects on *what* is being taught and learned and *who* is receiving what instruction." She concluded that a wide latitude of student course selection in high schools magnifies the social stratification of educational outcomes. "This socially undesirable consequence results from two well documented relationships: (a) following a more demanding set of academic courses in high school is strongly and positively associated with higher academic achievement and (b) less advantaged students are considerably less likely to select such a demanding course of study than their more academically and socially advantaged counterparts. Additionally, academically and socially disadvantaged students and their families are less likely to seek out, or to have access to, information about the consequences of their choices (of either schools or courses)" (Lee 1993:125).

In their 1992 paper, Plank, Schiller, Schneider, and Coleman found that the choice schools they studied drew families that were far less affluent than families who sent their children to private schools, somewhat less affluent than families who sent their children to assigned neighborhood schools, and more affluent than families who sent their children to magnet schools and vocational-technical schools. Choice schools were likely to have a larger proportion of minorities than private or neighborhood schools, and fewer minorities than magnet or vocational-technical schools. In terms of eighth-grade achievement, students in choice schools did not do as well as those in private and assigned neighborhood schools, but they did better than students in magnet and vocational-technical schools. This tells us that choice schools are somewhat more integrated than assigned schools and private schools, and that there is little indication of a devastating creaming effect on either the private schools or the local public schools. In terms of racial segregation, the authors conclude (1992:16) that their results "suggest that there are no uniformly integrative or segregative effects of public schools of choice as they exist in the American high school system today." To my mind, however, the risk that unregulated open-enrollment policies may create greater class and race segregation is substantial. Choice advocates often claim that the public school system is very segregated and that school choice policies could not possibly make it more so. I believe this claim is glib. Not only could the situation be worse, but if we remove the legal and moral barriers that have been erected against segregation, we will create a system of public and private schools that are divided by race and class. There is the distinct possibility that the ideal of the common school will evaporate from public consciousness.

Private School Choice and Equity

Because so few school choice plans include private schools, there is very little empirical evidence as to the consequences of including private schools in choice programs. Private schools, especially those that enroll students from high-status families, are able to pass on to their students what the sociologists Pierre Bourdieu and Jean-Claude Passeron (1977) call "cultural capital." Graduating from a private school confers a certain amount of social status. Much of the literature concerning private schools has been extremely naive because the authors have failed to take into account the distinction between educational amount and educational route. When a student enters the private sector, he or she is on a different educational route than a public school student. We know, for instance, that private school students attend more selective colleges than public school students, even when the students' academic achievements and family backgrounds are similar (Cookson 1981:157). We also know that there is a network that helps private school students gain admission to private selective colleges (Persell and Cookson

1985). Private schools are able to place "floors" under their weaker students; that is, average or below-average students are protected against downward educational mobility by the mere fact of having attended a private school (Cookson and Persell 1985; Persell, Catsambis, and Cookson 1992a and b).

Moreover, the higher the social status of the private school, the greater its effect in the secondary school–to-college transition. Private school attendance has a direct effect on students' educational mobility and thus tends to reproduce social-class and educational stratification. Socially and academically, elite private schools have internal characteristics and external connections that make them potent vehicles for creating and maintaining educational inequalities. These inequalities can last a lifetime, although it should be said that the elite schools do enroll a good number of disadvantaged students, for many of whom the advantages of graduating from an elite school can last a lifetime (Zweigenhaft and Domhoff 1991).

Not all private schools have so much social power, but it takes little imagination to see that large-scale private school systems such as those proposed by the founders of the Edison Project could have significant consequences on educational equity. These comments are not intended as an indictment of private education, but rather as recognition that in a highly stratified society it is quite likely that including private schools in choice plans will increase rather than decrease educational inequality. There is, however, one caveat to this conclusion that I will amplify in the final chapter. Private schools in the inner city perform a public service unlike other private schools. Without these schools we would lose an important resource in an already desperate situation. I believe that these schools deserve public support, not through a large-scale voucher plan, but through low-cost government loans and outright grants.

This brings us to the only real evidence we have concerning the impact on educational equity of a publicly funded private school choice plan. We have already seen that the Milwaukee choice program has not resulted in increased student achievement, but has it had any impact on equity? Witte (1992) has indicated that knowledge about the choice program is uneven and basically word-of-mouth, although we know that applications for the program increased from 577 in 1990–1991 to 998 in 1992–1993. Fifty-seven percent of choice parents reported being on public assistance, compared to 39 percent of other Milwaukee parents. Two-thirds of the students participating in the choice program are entitled to a free lunch. Choice families are more likely to be headed by a single parent than the average Milwaukee public school family, and nearly three-quarters of the families participating in the program are African-American. Consistent with other findings, choice mothers tend to be more highly educated than other mothers.

Only one percent of Milwaukee students may participate in the choice program, so it is hard to tell whether a large-scale private school choice plan elsewhere would have a significant impact on equity. In the first year of the Milwaukee program only seven schools participated, with one Montessori school enrolling only two choice children. Witte believes that the Milwaukee choice program offers an educational opportunity to students who are doing poorly in the public school system. He argues that parents participating in the program express greater satisfaction with their children's private schools than with their prior public schools. The Milwaukee experiment is too new and too small to tell us much about whether spending public funds for private schools would lead to greater educational inequalities. However, there are many Milwaukee-type proposals throughout the United States that, if enacted, would give us a much clearer idea about how private schools influence the life arithmetic of students.

School Choice and Community

One of the ironies of examining the outcomes of school choice is that the farther one gets from the technical core of instruction, the more significant the effects of choice appear. By this I mean that the process of choosing schools is perhaps more important than the measurable, tangible outcomes of school choice that so obsess the research community. Perhaps the most important outcome of school choice is the sense of ownership that students and families can have if they are able to choose schools creatively. Choice is a form of empowerment, an overused but nonetheless important term. There is something dignified about being allowed to choose a school rather than being compelled to attend a particular school.

We have already touched on this issue earlier. Parent information centers not only provide information about schools to parents, they also provide information about students to schools. The act of going to such a center is symbolically rich; families are integrated into their communities by participating in choice. In this sense, school choice, especially managed school choice, can be a breath of fresh air. Schools are required to open their doors to families and in doing so break down the barriers that have isolated schools from their communities and isolated parents from schools. Almost all research indicates that parent involvement in schooling is beneficial to students' cognitive and affective growth. There are no convincing studies about the global effects of school choice on community because these effects are not easily measured by traditional research methods. Community well-being is not a variable that can be easily included in statistical analyses; yet the global intangible effects of school choice are more likely to endure than are effects related to student achievement and perhaps even to school improvement.

Creating Social Trust

In this chapter we have asked the question, Does choice make a difference? We have found that in terms of student achievement, choice makes little difference. In terms of school improvement, choice has secondary effects that can raise the level of schools' academic climates. In terms of equity, we have found that, depending on the plan, choice can result in greater or less integration, or have very little effect at all. In other words, it is impossible to make general statements about the relationship of equity to choice without reference to specific plans. Finally, I have argued that choice has beneficial communal effects that are only marginally related to student achievement and school improvement. Schools are social organizations, and if they can influence families and communities to be more participatory, it makes sense to think of choice as a way of creating community. John E. Coons (1992) has written that school choice is based on social trust. If choice does indeed create more social trust, then it is an experiment worth pursuing, within the context of improving and transforming public education.

5 The Stark Utopia
The Market as Messiah

The public school system as we have known it is being transformed because the structure of American society and economy has been transformed and requires a system of public
education that is more flexible, more innovative, and more just.
As I see it, two competing metaphors will shape the public education system of the future. The first is that of democracy. At the
heart of the democratic relationship is the implicit or explicit
covenant: important human interactions are essentially communal. Democratic metaphors lead to a belief in the primacy
and efficacy of citizenship as a way of life. The second
metaphor is that of the market. At the heart of the market relationship is the implicit or explicit contract: human interactions
are essentially exchanges. Market metaphors lead to a belief in
the primacy and efficacy of consumership as a way of life.

In the final chapter we will examine the democratic
metaphor in some depth as it relates particularly to school
choice and educational reform. In this chapter we will examine

the market metaphor because it has come to dominate public discourse concerning educational reform. One need only read the front pages of the *New York Times* and the editorial pages of the *Wall Street Journal* to recognize that there is an emerging consensus that privatizing education will lead to an educational renaissance. This faith in markets needs to be analyzed critically because behind the rhetoric of consumership lie several highly questionable assumptions about human behavior and society. In particular, we will examine the emergence of "homo economicus" and the religious origins of market morality. We will also look at rational-choice theory as it applies to school choice: the belief that people are rational choosers and will select schools that are academically superior. Last, we will investigate how educational markets have operated internationally, so as to determine what evidence, if any, there is that market solutions to educational problems produce an educational renaissance.

I should say at the outset that there is a place for competition in education and that educational experiments that include market components may prove valuable in redesigning public education. But education is a human service, with emphasis on both *human* and *service*. In the words of the economist Karl Polanyi, markets make wonderful servants but terrible masters. The process of educating a child is not the same as building a car or selling advertising. Unregulated market practices in education could lead to a world of designer schools, offering trendy curricula and utilizing questionable pedagogic strategies. Moreover, markets do not work as well as their advocates claim; in particular, they punish the poor and often provide shoddy products. But why are markets so attractive now? Why do market-oriented school reformers speak of competition as though it were the magic panacea for educational ills? Why do educational free-marketers believe that choice and choice alone will create an educational wonderland? And why do these reformers ignore the role of culture and power in shaping human preferences? My experience in studying private schools has taught me that the assumptions many market advocates make about preference formation are conceptually thin and often naive.

The millenarian urge that underlies American beliefs about education's power to transform society has distorted our understanding of its true possibilities and limitations. The rise of the market model of educational reform partakes of this urge with a particularly modern, or perhaps postmodern, twist. In 1950 David Riesman, with his colleagues Nathan Glazer and Reuel Denney, published a now-classic book entitled *The Lonely Crowd: A Study of the Changing American Character.* In this critique of modern life, the authors contrast what they see as the older cultural archetype, the "inner-directed man," with the newer cultural archetype, "the outer-directed man." While the former constructed an inner reality based primarily on the hope for spiritual salvation, the latter constructs a social reality based on popular acceptance. The older millenarianism hypothesized a utopia in the afterlife; the newer millenarianism hypothesizes a utopia on earth. Its driving force is the market metaphor. What we own, what we consume, and what we can buy define who we are. And in a society as status-hungry as the United States, material success has come to be equated not only with social status but with personal worth.

Market-driven school choice is what might be called outer-directed school reform. It concerns itself not with the content of education but exclusively with its form. The belief that good schools are products of good choices is a utopian conception because it reifies the relationship between school and society and removes schools from their messy social contexts; real-world business practices are about marketing and selling products for a profit. These profits are not returned to society, except in the form of taxation; they are retained by businesses, individuals, and families. As we have seen, this has led to a huge disparity between the rich and the poor in the United States. How is it, then, that the market metaphor has become so popular? Why is it that a significant number of scholars and policymakers have advocated an ideology called rational-choice theory? What have been the effects of privatizing other human services in terms of accountability, convenience, and expense? And what can we learn from experiments with privatization and school choice in other countries?

The Emergence of Homo Economicus

With the election of Ronald Reagan in 1980, free enterprise and capitalism developed a new sense of purpose and legitimacy. Since the Great Depression capitalism had been on the defensive. Although it seems ancient history now, during the first two-thirds of the twentieth century, socialism in its hard and soft forms seemed to be the ascending political ideology. The American form of socialism was very soft indeed. America's welfare state, upon which so much abuse has been heaped, is pitifully small compared to that of most other industrialized countries. The older liberals proposed that society could be reformed through government action, and there was general consensus that the liberal reforms were producing a better society. The United States in the past twenty years, however, has undergone rapid social, economic, and technological changes. The liberal world view has grown timid and ineffective. In the meantime, liberals have been challenged by a variety of political conservatives, including the new right.

The new right is a political movement that primarily finds its strength west of the Mississippi and south of the Mason-Dixon Line. While some new right groups are profoundly antigovernment and even marginal to mainstream American life, most of the new conservatives are, in the words of Sen. Barry Goldwater of Arizona, "fairly well-to-do people . . . very sincere in their beliefs." Goldwater prophesied the coming of a conservative political messiah, although he may not have guessed that this messiah would take the form of a Hollywood actor. Goldwater believes in a rough-and-ready America where people are rewarded according to individual effort, where government is minimal and the military is powerful. With his defeat in the presidential election of 1964, the liberal coalition seemed secure. But by the end of the 1970s, the economic and social environment of the United States had made the liberal coalition politically vulnerable.

Reagan expressed an ideology of social Darwinism that echoed Goldwater's individualism, but with an easygoing acceptance of human foibles. Unlike Goldwater, Reagan was able to capture the middle-class vote as well as the traditional conservative vote, and he came to Washington ready to downsize government. He was also ready to revise the tax code to accommodate his most powerful supporters, wealthy people eager to change the rules regarding capital gains. The effect of Reagan's presidency was profound. By cutting social benefits and reducing the capital gains tax, he precipitated a dramatic shift of income and wealth to the upper-middle and upper classes. An almost permanent underclass emerged during the 1980s.

Riding on Reagan's coattails were a good number of disaffected intellectuals who found the liberal world view to be anathema. One has the feeling that many of them would like to roll back the calendar and begin the Enlightenment all over again. They are essentially Burkean conservatives who are skeptical about the morality and efficacy of the social contract and believe that social progress can be brought about only through competition. During the 1980s many of these conservative intellectuals came to Washington and set up foundations, think tanks, and cultural forums that are interlinked, interdependent, and ideologically committed. In effect, they have established a conservative infrastructure that is a far cry from the philosophy of Barry Goldwater. The new conservatives are well aware of public relations, organizationally adroit, and politically savvy. They believe in the basic principles of eighteenth-century capitalism: individualism, competition, and profit. Whereas liberals and radicals have relentlessly critiqued American culture as materialistic and American business practices as exploitive, this new power élite rejoices in the triumph of capitalism and its many manifestations. Whereas materialism in the liberal world view is treated as a nasty little secret, acquisition in the new conservative world order has attained the status of religious fulfillment. These beliefs form the core of the New Paradigm, which is essentially old-fashioned individualism in a white shirt and a Gucci tie, with a lap-top computer.

All this is very curious, because capitalism in the United States has evolved not in opposition to the state but in cooperation with it; advanced capitalism is deeply enmeshed with the apparatus of government. Even a cursory knowledge of the relationship between federal regulatory agencies and large businesses demonstrates that the megacorporation is hardly an example of eighteenth-century capitalism. The idea that government has hindered the growth of corporations and multinationals is out of keeping with reality. The advocates of the New Paradigm, however, tend to ignore the fact that big business and big government are at least first cousins, if not more closely related. They create a somewhat imaginary world of individual entrepreneurs producing marvelous new products that would sell like mad if only the government would get off their backs. This idealized depiction of capitalism is often reflected in the literature on market-driven school choice.

It is not surprising that advocates of the New Paradigm should turn their attention to educational reform. After all, education is the country's largest business, and education is a social issue that will not go away. What better place to attack the liberal establishment than in its fortress of public education? As public confidence in public education declined, the intellectual scouts of the New Paradigm saw the opportunity to create an educational system compatible with their beliefs. An early prophet of capitalism in education is Myron Lieberman, who believes that the only way to improve American education is to "(1) foster private schools that compete with public schools and among themselves and/or (2) foster for-profit competition among service providers within the public school system" (1989:4).

Entrepreneurship in the public sector may be a mixed blessing. Choice and marketing in principle are very different; in reality they are nearly indistinguishable. As choice becomes an increasingly popular educational reform, some educational entrepreneurs may see it as a method of advancing themselves as well as of improving schools. Because market-oriented choice encourages risk taking and the rejection of the educational status quo, it is naive to think that education will not attract adventurous administrators who may be strong in sales but weak in educational philosophy and administrative expertise. The case of Walter Marks is instructive on this point. As superintendent of schools in Richmond, California, from 1987 to 1990, Marks introduced a choice plan that was innovative but too expensive for the school district. He was fired for incurring a debt of $19 million. Marks was excellent at self-promotion and had a $61,000 video made to promote his program for school choice in which he is referred to as a "miracle worker."

Apparently, Marks did not feel accountable to the traditional administrative values of the educational establishment. Such a position has an appeal because so much of the establishment seems to resist change. The tradition is worth preserving, however, because administrators' skills are developed in a supervised environment where accountability and prudence are emphasized. In managing school systems, these two virtues are essen-

tial: the lives of children should not be dependent on the schemes of administrators. Marketing strategies for schools are not the same thing as genuine
curricular or pedagogical reforms. Today, we are being told by such
respectable sources as the *Wall Street Journal* that competition and markets
will save America's schools, but history shows us that in an unregulated market, cleverness and cunning can be used to market products and services that
are expensive, shoddy, and even harmful to human and intellectual health.

The Religious Origins of Market Morality

We have seen earlier that there is an evangelical Protestant component to
the school choice coalition that is fervent in its rejection of compulsory
public education. The historical linkage between Protestantism and capitalism is intimate. While many Catholics support school choice as a prag-
matic way of financially saving their schools, the world view of the most
avid and ideological school choice supporters has its origins in the linkage
between Protestant individualism and the social philosophy underlining
capitalism. Perhaps this is what gives the market-driven school choice
movement its particular cultural flavor: one part resentment, one part spiritual fervor, one part frank acquisitiveness.

There are few topics over which scholars have spilled more ink than the
origins of capitalism. The transition of European economies to capitalism
in the nineteenth century was one of the great transformations in world history, and, as the sociologist Max Weber has shown, the driving energy of
capitalism springs in good part from a religious orientation. Protestantism,
especially in its evangelical Calvinist form, openly questions the proposi-
tion that the meek shall inherit the earth and that poverty is a sign of spiritual grace. According to Calvin, individuals are responsible for their own
salvation. The importance of a religiously sanctioned radical individualism
as an organizing metaphor for personal and social relationships cannot be
overstated (Bellah et al. 1987). As an ideology it has shaped public institutions; as a belief system it defines and regulates our commitments and
values; and its root metaphor gives coherence to the capitalist world view.

Those who have thought deeply about the social psychology of capitalism have differed significantly in interpreting its effects on human behavior. For some, capitalism has freed the human spirit and encourages initiative, thrift, and diligence. For others, capitalism has created a deep alienation within and between individuals. But whether one praises the spirit of capitalism or condemns it, there can be little doubt that a key component of the capitalist way of thinking is calculation based on perceived self-interest. The pursuit of self-interest requires individuals to view human relationships as a form of exchange. We establish relationships in order to benefit ourselves, and we hope to receive more than we can give, because it is in that type of exchange that surpluses, symbolic and real, are accumulated. We enter into the social contract in the hope of becoming rich and in doing so come to view human relationships in terms of supply and demand. In this sense, capitalism cannot escape its own logic of commodification.

The political scientist Mancur Olson, Jr., in *The Logic of Collective Action: Public Goods and the Theory of Groups* (1965), makes the argument that group efforts contain within them a fundamental contradiction. If I enhance the well-being of the group, I may well diminish my own personal opportunities. Ultimately, the rationale for sacrificing for the good of the group runs counter to the belief in individualism. This may explain, in part, why such collective organizations as labor unions have not been successful in ridding their members of the social psychology of capitalism, which tells us that in the end it's a Hobbesian world of all against all. Capitalism has proved effective in producing material abundance for some people, at least in Europe, the United States, and Japan. In countries where there is a cultural and material infrastructure that allows for initiative, there is little doubt that market economies produce many goods for those who can afford them. Whether capitalism produces a compassionate and good society is a more controversial issue. Nonetheless, we are living in an era where capitalism seems to have survived the socialist threat and feels itself triumphant. If an individual fails in a capitalistic society, it is not the society's shortcomings that are held accountable but the individual's.

Clearly, the capitalistic world view is present in the school choice movement. It is the social gestalt that gives the movement its energy and cohesion.

In this way of thinking, students become consumers and schools become educational producers. It is the student's responsibility to find a good school, and it is the school's responsibility to deliver the expected educational product. This way of thinking shifts the onus of educational responsibility from the school to the student. In debates on school choice I have often heard it said that what this movement is all about is giving poor children the same opportunities as rich children. If rich children can go to private schools, why shouldn't poor children do likewise? This position has all the characteristics of a straw man. Capitalism cannot be magically removed from the class system; individuals' opportunities are structured by their social-class positions. Moreover, many market-oriented school choice advocates describe the process of choosing as "rational." Do people rationally choose such consumption items as automobiles, televisions, and houses? Do people rationally choose their spouses? What does "rational" mean in the face of psychoanalytic theory? Are we confusing reason with the price system?

The Social Construction of Reason

Since the Enlightenment, reason has been elevated to the pantheon of human virtues. To refer to an individual as reasonable implies that he or she is not controlled by emotions and is able to think in a logical, sequential manner. People who make decisions based on reason are thought to be wise. Reason is akin to calculation, but nobler. The identification of reason with economic self-interest has produced a way of thinking that has come to characterize the Western mind in particular. The cultural institutionalization of reason has resulted in a school of thought called rational-choice theory. Essentially, the theory hypothesizes that social actors will make choices among alternatives in such a way as to maximize their utility. One of the most eloquent proponents of rational-choice theory is the sociologist James S. Coleman, a school choice advocate.

Sophisticated rational-choice theorists such as Coleman do not argue that rational choice occurs in a vacuum; they recognize that power relations influence the choices people make, and also that the economic metaphor underlying the theory of rational choice is inadequate to explain all of human behavior. Still, rational-choice theorists do believe in the power of self-interest to create rational and just societies. According to the sociologist David Sciulli (1991:2–8), rational choice rests on five linked assumptions:

1. Individual actors are typically dedicated to maximizing their own private "wealth."

2. Actors' subjective interests or desired ends are ultimately "sovereign," both conceptually and in practice. Actors need not justify their preferences with either normative or cognitive rationales.

3. Society's existing distribution of rights and duties is treated as given, or as random.

4. Actors' relatively unfettered efforts to maximize their own private wealth are likely to result in collective prosperity or social wealth.

5. Actors' relatively unfettered pursuit of their own preferences is more likely to yield and sustain a benign direction of social change —a stable liberal-democratic society—than any effort to restrain this pursuit with institutionalized norms.

These assumptions are at the very center of the argument that, given the opportunity, individuals will choose the best schools for their children. The question is, do individuals make decisions in the manner described above, especially outside the economic realm? Certainly, rational-choice theory can be challenged from a psychoanalytic point of view, whether or not one has a Freudian orientation. Any number of unconscious reasons and motivations may impel individuals to make certain choices. Every human being's perceptions, beliefs, and attitudes are the product of many life experiences, some remembered, some forgotten. The human brain itself is a complex mechanism that channels our responses in particular ways.

Human decision-making processes are certainly not based on reason alone. Some wits have suggested that economics is all about the choices people have and that sociology tells us that people have no choices at all. Economists tend to minimize the importance of culture, habit, tradition, roles, and duty in shaping human preferences, while sociologists sometimes can be faulted for creating an image of human behavior that excludes free will. Another way of putting this is to distinguish between what the economist Herbert Simon has called objective rationality and subjective rationality. He writes (1987:39): "In situations that are complex and in which information is very incomplete (i.e., virtually all real world situations), the behavior theories deny that there is any magic for producing behavior even approximating an objective maximization of profits or utilities. They therefore seek to determine what the actual frame of the decision is, how that frame arises from the decision situation, and how, within that frame, reason operates."

In Simon's parlance, "the frame of decision" includes any number of subjective perceptions reinforced by incomplete information. The sociologist Amy Stuart Wells (1991), in a study of a suburban/urban desegregation plan in St. Louis that included a choice component, interviewed African-American families about their reasons for choosing or not choosing one of several predominantly white schools in the suburbs. She discovered that for many African-Americans, race is such an important issue that it often supersedes evaluations of academic programs; that is, discrimination is so institutionalized in American culture that decision-making processes for African-Americans are almost always bound by their perceptions of the larger society. Some parents, faced with the choice between an academically outstanding school and a school that was racially homogeneous, chose the latter because they were concerned about their children's self-esteem. Studies by Willms and Echols (1992) have also shown that in Scotland students and families often choose schools for nonacademic reasons.

Rational-choice theory is an extremely abstract set of propositions that are logically interrelated but generally unsupported empirically. The historian David Hogan has written cogently about the relationship between rational-choice theory and the creation of educational markets. "As a theory about the nature of choice under very strict conditions, the theory is not without its arcane uses and interest in theoretical models of competitive markets. But as a descriptive or explanatory theory of the real world of the educational marketplace, it leaves much to be desired. In particular, it provides a much too 'thin' account of the nature of social action. In order to do greater justice to the complexity and embeddedness of parental choice, we need a much thicker theory of social action." Hogan goes on to analyze the components of a "thicker theory" of social action, which specifies the elements of what might be called a social and cultural theory of educational choice. The notion of individual preferences is deeply embedded in culture. In fact, cultural necessities are often experienced as psychological constructs. What real people define as utility is the product of their social position and the social space they occupy. According to Hogan, "It is quite clear that most people, most of the time, do not make the kind of decisions that would satisfy the formal requirements of perfect rationality in rational choice theory and, indeed, could not" (Hogan 1991:3,5). Rationality is bounded because it is embedded in the evolution of the human species and the cultural contexts of decision makers.

In applying the theory of rational choice to the issue of school choice, we come face to face with the issue of social class and other forms of social stratification. Individuals and groups are not only stratified by income, wealth, race, ethnicity, and gender, they are also stratified by their values, and these values are directly related to their social-class position. Consciousness itself is stratified. The class structure of any industrialized society influences profoundly how and what people think. All choices are situationally bound and can never be "rational." In the United States, the significance of social class is generally underestimated because the existence of permanent social classes undermines the myth of individualism. Power relationships create choices, shape preferences, and influence decision making. We know that different classes have different attitudes about the value of education (MacLeod 1987; Persell and Cookson 1992). For the upper class, education is an important status symbol, primarily because of its ornamental value. For the upper-middle class, education defines status and provides individuals with credentials that are needed in the professional and business arenas. For the middle class, education is the gateway to respectability. And for the working and underclass, education is of marginal utility in terms of social mobility. Bourdieu and others have shown convincingly that educational attainment is contingent on how much cultural capital a student "inherits" from his or her home. Schools transmit status in ways that have little to do with formal curricula and pedagogies.

Before I ever heard the expression "cultural capital," I learned this lesson when I worked as a teacher and administrator in a private school. The social-class backgrounds of the students in this school were, on average, higher than those of the students in the public school where I had previously taught. But was the private school a better school than the public school? Actually, no. The private school had an extremely traditional curriculum. Most of the teachers who were my colleagues were amateurs in the sense that they had received no formal training in education and were headed toward other careers. The resources of the school were minimal, and its administration was not noticeably effective. So, why did the parents of the private school students spend thousands of dollars each year to avoid sending their children to the local public schools, which, on the face of it, were superior to the private school? One father summed this up for me: "What you get here are the other parents." It was the status characteristics of the private school that made it so desirable to ambitious parents. Were the choices these parents made rational? From an academic point of view, no. From a social point of view, yes. Rational-choice theories that ignore the significance of social stratification and the symbolic importance of cultural capital treat preference formation as though it occurred in a social vacuum. This is a dangerous intellectual blind spot because if we do not recognize the structural inequalities that shape educational decision making, we are likely to produce educational systems that increase inequality rather than provide channels of mobility for youngsters from poor and disadvantaged homes.

We are both the products and the agents of history. There is a dialectical relationship between the collective decisions individuals make and the larger social structure. In this sense, preference formation is interactive and recursive. Society shapes our preferences before we make them, but we can influence the choices available to us by our exercise of preferences. There is nothing linear or uncomplicated about the processes by which people choose schools, and there is very little that is rational about preference formation. Rational choice is a kind of grand illusion of order in what is, in fact, a complicated, power-oriented, and sometimes chaotic world. In sum, the theory of rational choice is an economic theory that may be applicable to price structures and even, to some degree, to supply and demand, but it is far too simplistic to cover all human decision-making processes. Human beings are often impulsive, petty, and stubborn, especially when it comes to their children. In the final analysis, the psychological characteristics of human beings and the social constraints placed on them by culture and power, make the theory of rational choice unconvincing at best.

Educational Markets and International Educational Reform

To those who believe in the power of the marketplace to create productive and just schools and societies, the 1980s must have seemed like the dawn of a new era. The yuppy revolution in the United States took place within the context of an international resurgence of conservative social policies and the collapse of the Soviet Union. The acquisition of money, which had previously been treated as a necessity, became celebrated as a social and moral achievement. Huge fortunes were made in the media and financial markets in the 1980s, and it is not by chance that the television show *Life Styles of the Rich and Famous* was enormously successful. Throughout the world the old models of education seemed hopelessly out of date as the promise of education for democracy and affluence turned sour (Cookson, Sadovnik, and Semel 1992). As the educational analyst Philip H. Coombs (1985:13–14) has observed, "The aura of euphoria that surrounded all things that are educational in the earlier Age of Innocence has now been transmuted into a crisis of confidence." This crisis of confidence goes very deep because it is education that is meant to rescue the world from poverty, racism, and injustice. Research repeatedly shows, however, that the links between educational and economic outcomes are weak, despite our deep faith that better schools lead to better jobs and higher productivity (Jencks et al. 1972, Berg 1971). The reality is that what one learns in school has little to do directly with one's earning power, but what one learns in school and where one goes to school have a great deal to do with one's social class of origin and of destination. Schools have been weak in producing numerate and literate students, but they have been strong in sorting students by social class, race, ethnicity, and gender. By and large, schools reinforce existing inequalities.

It is not surprising, therefore, that the 1980s was a period of international disillusionment about the power of education to solve social problems. The response to this disillusionment among political leaders was not to reflect on education's limited power to transform society (if, in fact, that was what was desired), but to redouble their efforts to use education as a rhetorical bulwark against the rising tide of mediocrity. As we have seen, the idea of restructuring school systems became increasingly fashionable in the United States as internal reforms proved ineffective. In Great Britain, conservatives began to attack the very nature of public or state education. Liberals, progressives, and radicals also began to examine alternate, more flexible ways of organizing public education.

School choice, or, as it is sometimes called internationally, parental choice, began to catch on in diverse countries, including Great Britain, France, Poland, Canada, Australia, and Israel. In one form or another, each of these countries created policies that heightened competition among schools and gave increasing credibility to the power of the marketplace to renew education. Under the aegis of the U.S. Department of Education, Charles Glenn published a book called *Choice of Schools in Six Nations* (1989)—France, Holland, Belgium, Britain, Canada, and Germany. Not surprisingly, Glenn views the international evidence as resoundingly supportive of school choice because liberty and fairness require it. Not only does choice provide, in Glenn's view, equal educational access for minorities, but it also has a positive effect on the quality of schooling available. The book has a foreword by former Secretary of Education Lauro F. Cavazos, the same man who organized choice forums throughout the United States during his tenure in office. Cavazos claims that choice leads to better schools and improved student learning.

The text itself is less about school choice than it is about private schools, particularly religious schools. According to Glenn, religious schools have played an important role in history because they have resisted governmental attempts to establish a state monopoly in education and, thus, a state monopoly over children's minds. Whereas the traditional historical view has pictured universal education as a necessity for public enlightenment, Glenn generally portrays religious and private schools as embattled bastions of liberty against the encroachments of a godless state.

In a curious inversion of the larger reality, private schools in this scenario become the true common schools, rooted in their communities, while public schools become the educational extensions of a cold and impersonal state. There is much to commend Glenn's work, but we must be extremely skeptical of histories and sociologies that divide the world along the lines he suggests. In fact, the international evidence concerning school choice cannot be very comforting to its advocates. While international comparisons must be treated with some skepticism because societies and cultures vary so widely, we can, in a brief overview, get some idea of how educational marketplaces have affected education in those countries that have experimented with choice.

The Netherlands, for instance, has one of the most extensive school choice systems in the world. Slightly larger than Maryland, with a population of fourteen million, the Netherlands is unique in that "educational and most other social services are financed by the government but are generally operated by private non-profit organizations, often religious in nature" (Brown 1992:177). The national constitution provides public support for religious schools, and establishing a private school in Holland is relatively easy. A group of parents, usually with the assistance of their church, petitions the government for a school. If the request is granted, the government pays all costs on a per-pupil basis, and the municipality provides the building for the school. According to Brown (1992:178), the Dutch system has not resulted in the kind of school system envisioned by many American choice advocates:

> What can we learn from school choice in the Netherlands? Parents may choose any school for their child but private schools may select from among applicants. There is less social conflict over education, and experimentation is possible but is rarely found in Dutch schools. Curriculum, pedagogy, and school organization are generally uniform throughout the country. Religious affiliation and residence are the strongest factors influencing school choice. Less popular schools do not disappear as market incentives would indicate. Pedagogy is in the hands of professional educators, with almost no parental participation. Parents determine a school's quality more on the visible social-

economic mixture of students and less on a school's academic performance. All schools, public and private, must follow rigid central government regulations on the curriculum but pedagogy is left to teachers. All students must take a national exam at the end of elementary school and at the end of high school. Teacher salaries, teacher credentials, and working conditions are regulated by the central government.

Moreover, Brown found that "white flight" is prevalent and that tracking takes place at age twelve via a required national examination which results in academic sorting by social class (1992:177–78). In short, the work of Brown should warn us that we must be careful to distinguish between the rhetoric and the reality of school choice when examining even so sophisticated a system as that in the Netherlands.

Evidence from Canada and Australia is also not reassuring. Donald Erickson (1986), a specialist in Canadian private schools, found that when the government funded private schools, they lost a great deal of their autonomy; moreover, public support of private schools did not lead to increased innovation or diversity. In effect, when private schools receive public funds, they become similar to public schools. This finding is of critical importance because too often advocates of school choice seem unaware that what distinguishes private from public schools is not the former's competitiveness but their autonomy. One of the ironies of intersectional school choice is that rather than increasing educational diversity, such policies may result in decreasing educational options. Since 1973 the Australians have also experimented with school choice. Private schools receive public funding. The poorer schools receive more funds than the relatively wealthy schools. Researchers have found that choice in Australia leads to a "creaming-off process." Upper-middle-class students tend to leave government secondary schools; this harms the reputation of the state schools and leads to further race and class stratification. Given what we know about the relationship between school and society, this is not a surprising outcome; students from wealthier homes have more educational alternatives and will tend to group together. The Australian case provides intriguing evidence that unless choice is carefully managed to ensure open access, school systems can be restratified and resegregated through open-enrollment policies.

School choice has become part of the public-policy agenda in a number of other countries. The government of François Mitterand of France was nearly toppled in the early 1980s when Mitterand suggested that public subsidies to Catholic schools be reduced or eliminated. In fact, France has been experimenting with school choice for over thirty years (Fowler 1992). In the end, however, the French system remains highly centralized. In eastern Europe and the former Soviet Union, a variety of school choice options is developing. For instance, after decades of Soviet domination, Polish communities and religious groups are creating a network of alternate schools that reflect local culture and traditions. In Israel school choice has become a national controversy. Traditional Israeli conceptions of a unified and unifying state school system are now being challenged by educational entrepreneurs who wish to sell their academic products. As in the United States, school choice in Israel touches on fundamental issues concerning the relationship between equity and liberty, and, as in the United States, marketplace freedom has been raised as a banner in favor of school choice.

By far the most extensive and daring experiments in school choice have occurred in Great Britain (Walford 1992). Although the Labour party had discussed various choice options prior to 1979, with the election of Margaret Thatcher as prime minister, school choice became a major educational initiative. The 1980 Education Act emphasized the need to generate more competition among schools. In 1982 parents were given the right to "express a preference" for a school and the local educational authorities were obliged to take this preference into account in assigning students to schools. At the same time, Scotland was also experimenting with increased parental choice. Families there are permitted to choose schools outside their school catchment area; during the 1980s the Scottish choice plan was more liberal than those in England and Wales. The Scottish plan made it very difficult for local educational authorities to restrict students' right to choose, although studies of the plan reveal that relatively few families placed requests for transfers. By the mid-1980s, only 9 percent of Scottish children at the elementary and secondary levels entered schools other than

116

the local one they would normally have attended. Urban families are far more likely to exercise choice than rural families, which seldom have the opportunity because of transportation problems. Researchers found that almost nobody wanted to transfer into a school in a working-class neighborhood. Two observations can be made about choice in Scotland: first, roughly 90 percent of parents do not exercise their right of choice, and thus the plan has few educational design implications; second, because of the marked tendencies of families to choose schools in middle-class neighborhoods, there is a distinct probability that unregulated choice will result in a two-tier system of education. The top tier will educate middle-class and mobile working-class students, and the bottom tier will educate less ambitious working-class students and students from the underclass.

In England and Wales school choice was expanded in the 1980s. Part of the 1980 Education Act was the "assisted placement scheme." This policy not only awarded private school tuition to individual families but gave direct financial and ideological support to the private schools. Research by Fitz, Edwards, and Whitty (1986) leaves little doubt that the scheme has primarily resulted in providing financial aid to middle-class families, since it is these families that are sought after by private schools. Moreover, there is some evidence that boys benefited more than girls (Walford 1992). Throughout the 1980s the Conservative government supported free enterprise as part of its effort to "roll back the frontiers of socialism." In 1986 the Conservatives announced a new and dramatic educational policy by establishing a pilot network of twenty city technical colleges. These are private schools funded by the government but run by educational trusts with close links to industry and commerce. They are meant to become "beacons of excellence." While the Conservative government genuinely desires to improve technical education, it is apparent that another purpose of the city technical colleges is to weaken the comprehensive state system of education and reduce the power of the local educational authorities (Walford 1992). The 1988 Educational Reform Act for England and Wales was a direct attempt to spread the privatization process within education. The purpose of the act was to increase competition among schools and to encourage parents to make choices. Schools can opt out of local authority control and become directly funded by the Department of Education and Science. Funding for local authority schools is now directly related to enrollment, so that popular schools receive proportionately larger amounts of funding. Thus schools will flourish or fall depending on the decisions that a relatively few families make within a short period.

This brief review does not do justice to the variety of choice plans that have been experimented with outside the United States. It will be particularly interesting to follow the development of the educational systems that emerge in the former Soviet Union and eastern Europe. It does appear that a significant number of parents throughout Europe and elsewhere wish to send their children to nonstate schools. Educational freedom is an important right that needs protection under the law. There is little evidence thus far, however, that market models of educational reform lead to innovative schools and school systems. Moreover, the international evidence seems to indicate that privatization and free choice lead to further social and educational stratification. This only reinforces what I think is the accurate perception that discussions about competition and choice that do not consider the social context may well create a rationale for school systems that produce more inequality and further educational and social injustices.

The Partial Panacea

We have examined the market metaphor of school reform from several perspectives. We have touched on the cultural and political context within which the market metaphor has become credible, and we have attempted to understand the relationship between individualism and the "sanctity of choice." Serious questions have been raised about rational choice as it pertains to how people choose in general and how they choose schools in particular. Last, we have seen that, on the basis of international experiments with privatization and choice, there are good reasons to be skeptical about the efficacy of markets to bring about meaningful and just educational change.

All this is not to say that competition among schools is unhealthy or unproductive. Certainly, schools should be accountable to students, families, and communities. Moreover, it needs to be reiterated and openly acknowledged that until the large-scale bureaucracies that strangle inner-city schools are dismantled, there is little hope for an educational renaissance in our cities. Market-oriented choice, however, is only a small part of a larger plan to create more vibrant school systems; genuine reform must spring from two sources: (1) a vision of inclusion and democracy, and (2) a vision of what constitutes a caring but rigorous learning environment. The market model of educational reform creates the image of a cool and dispassionate world of so-called rational choosers. This is a stark utopia that is neither desirable nor possible. Human behavior cannot be reduced to a mathematical formula. Market solutions to educational problems will not lead to educational wonderlands but could quite possibly lead to educational wastelands. Without accountability there is a danger that families will receive shoddy educational products and may be defrauded by unscrupulous operators masquerading as educators. In the next chapter, we will investigate the democratic metaphor of educational reform and the role choice can play in creating a more innovative, egalitarian school system.

6 Reinventing Public Education

The profound issues facing American education are not likely to be resolved through school choice alone because student enrollment policies do not address the question of educational purpose or the social problems that are literally destroying many American children. Schools may not transform society, but schools can transform the lives of children; schools are social interventions as well as social inventions. For too long we have viewed education as a contractual relationship. The nature of this relationship is made most explicit by market advocates who speak of "educational products" as though an education were something that could be manufactured and consumed. The meaning of the verb *educate* is to "draw out," not to "put in." Learning is not something we can buy; it is something we must experience.

The challenge of education is to develop in children a sense of active engagement with themselves. True education is about values, beliefs, and attitudes. There is much in our society that challenges the wholesomeness that should be our legacy to the next generation. To put the matter somewhat differently, we are challenged to choose between the fragmented consciousness of the modern materialistic mind and the humanistic vision of the whole empathetic and productive mind. We need a transcendent view of education, the elements of which include individual responsibility, the centrality of individual worth, equality, peace, and the primacy of the child's physical, intellectual, and spiritual rights. In short, education ought to be reclaimed, reinvented, and re-enchanted. The education of the future should engage the mind, touch the heart, and kindle the spirit.

"Inner-Directed" School Reform

As I have mentioned, school choice is an "outer-directed" school reform; that is, its advocates ask us to believe that if we attend to the governance and the form of schooling, the purpose of schooling will somehow magically take care of itself. In this chapter, I suggest that we need an "inner-directed" school reform movement that addresses the real needs of children and is committed to the preservation of democracy, the advancement of social justice, and the creation of schools that are oases of hope and intellectual ferment. This inner-directed school reform is based on a social covenant that states that every child, regardless of family background, has a right to health, safety, decent shelter, nourishment, and the best education we can offer. This covenant is based on trust and a commitment to the future. School choice does have a role to play in this transformation, but only insofar as it is tied to the knowledge that without purpose and direction, reform is like a rudderless ship in a storm of conflicting opinion.

Below we will examine the essential elements of a new educational covenant and what this covenant implies for the creation of dynamic, caring, and productive schools. This perspective is incorporated in a specific plan for educational reform built around three fundamental policy postulates: every child is entitled to an educational trust fund that ensures equality of educational opportunity, managed school choice, and the creation of model schools. We must balance instrumental approaches to school reform with expressive approaches if we are to nurture children and young people. Nurturing is the key to genuine educational reform. I hope we can create schools that are based on trust and warmth, not schools that glorify competition and coldness. Schools must be antidotes to the addictive, depressive culture that is robbing children of their vitality and hope. Schools can play an important role in moving society toward an era of community and communion.

Allan Shedlin, Jr., Gordon J. Klopf, and Esther S. Zaret at the National Elementary School Center, a child-advocacy and policy organization in New York City, argue that elementary schools must "function as a locus of advocacy for all children in the school. . . . We see the elementary school, working in collaboration with families and community, as the strategic agency to serve as brokers and advocates on the behalf of children. School, after all, is where the children are" (National Elementary School Center 1992:2). The center conceptualizes what children need today in three categories: survival needs, needs for belonging, and "thrival" needs. These categories are similar to those created by the United Nations Convention on Children's Rights: the right to survival, the right to protection, and the right to develop. The rights apply not only to children in elementary schools but to young people at the secondary level as well. And they apply to all children, no matter what their family background, academic capacities, or future possibilities.

The National Elementary School Center defines children's and young people's needs as follows:

> *Survival needs* identify the child's requirements for protection and a safe environment—in school and out; for the fundamental life skills to function in society; and for attention to the child's unique patterns of development and learning.

> *Needs for belonging* identify the child's requirements to be part of a primary nurturing unit; to have a sense of competency and self-worth; to receive acknowledgment and support of his or her independence and uniqueness; to have support in developing interdependent relationships with peers and adults; and to enjoy respect for his or her heritage: racial, ethnic, social, and family lifestyle.

Thrival needs identify the child's requirements for continuing personal, intellectual, and social growth, and for continuing development as a participating and contributing member in school life and in the broader social context.

Society has an obligation to meet the hunger needs of its youngest citizens. Unless children's basic physical, emotional, intellectual, and spiritual hungers are met, they will not develop the basic sense of trust in themselves and in society that is prerequisite to active citizenship, economic productivity, and personal development. Anyone who has spent time in schools can tell you that children's needs for attachment and fulfillment are so basic and so powerful that when they are unmet they can literally make children crazy. Above all, children have a hunger to communicate. Communication is essential for the social organization of the mind. Without communication we psychically starve to death. Schools of the future must be nourishing institutions that meet the hunger needs of children. This implies social trust and sharing, which in turn create the conditions for the unfolding of democracy.

Schools as Oases of Authenticity

Robert Bellah and his associates (1987) have discussed in depth how the cult of individualism has undermined our sense of community and civic responsibility. Certainly, market beliefs about educational reform promote self-interest over social commitment and attempt to create communities where lifestyle loyalties supersede community loyalties. Society is not a mere collection of individuals. The building blocks of society are groups with different amounts and forms of power. Democracy is a mechanism for protecting those with the least power and for peacefully negotiating differences between groups. Learning the rules of this negotiation process is essential if democracy is to survive. Schools therefore must create the conditions where children internalize the values and rules of democracy if society is not to be torn apart by competing interests and oppressed by those who have the most power. There is something paradoxical about those who are concerned about the public school monopoly but seem indifferent to the monopoly of wealth and power that characterizes so much of American life.

In order to revitalize public education, schools must be transformed into communities of learning. School choice must be real choice. What difference does the right to choose schools make if the schools from which students and parents may choose are inadequate or destructive? A key question in the debate concerning school choice is whether choice can improve the supply of schools available to families. Mary Anne Raywid has argued that choice can lead to school improvement and learning environments that are not "soft jails." Joe Nathan has also argued that choice encourages creative alternatives to the traditional neighborhood school. But one of the arguments against school choice, especially private school choice, is that without centralized control and accountability, some groups and individuals would found schools based on undemocratic principles. According to this scenario, the American public school system would be replaced by a balkanized public and private school system. Experience shows that without accountability there is a danger that "designer" schools would flourish (Kozol 1992).

Trying to balance innovation with accountability requires the agility of a tightrope walker, although I believe it can be done. There is little evidence that school choice automatically leads to the foundation of bizarre schools. In fact, most alternative public schools have been founded by public school educators who have a deep commitment to children and find that the conventional public school system stifles creativity. We have already seen that it was Anthony Alvarado's decision to let teachers found their own schools that led to the creation of a choice system in East Harlem. New York City has been experimenting with school choice for a number of years, particularly in District 4, in District 2, which covers Midtown and the Upper East Side of Manhattan, and in District 1, on the Lower East Side. In 1992 former Schools Chancellor Joseph Fernandez instituted a system that essentially allows children in the city to pick any elementary school of their choice (Berger 1992a). What evidence is there that choice in these districts improves the supply of schools that are available to families?

When William E. Urbinas arrived as superintendent of schools of District 1 in 1990, he discovered that the schools of the Lower East Side were "hemorrhaging" students, who were leaving District 1 and enrolling in the newly established experimental schools of District 2. The superintendent of schools in District 2 is Anthony Alvarado, former superintendent of District 4. In 1987 District 1 had 10,006 students; in 1991 it had 8,966. According to Urbinas, District 1 was becoming a "dying" district. He began several educational innovations of his own, including the Neighborhood School at P.S. 63, modeled after the ideas of Deborah Meier and her colleagues. The Neighborhood School has many of the characteristics of a progressive school. Children do not work from workbooks, and correct spelling is not raised to a level of obsession. Other schools in District 1 have begun to experiment with curricula and teaching techniques, and the parents of District 1 have expressed their faith in the new schools by not sending their children to other school districts in the city. The educational philosophies that shape the programs of many public schools of choice tend to be progressive rather than traditional. The reason for this, I believe, is that creative educators, especially at the elementary school level, view education from the point of view of child development. Teachers teach children first and subjects second; it is highly likely that if controlled school choice were implemented in the public sector there would be a growth of relatively small progressive schools.

Moreover, there is little evidence from the private sector that parents will choose schools that advocate hatred or follow policies that are not in the best interest of children. The overwhelming majority of parents love their children and would not spend months searching for schools that they believe would be destructive to their children. Schools that did not provide students with skills would also not last long. Americans are convinced that education is the key to social and economic mobility. In addition, although children may have different learning styles, learning itself is a predictable process. There is not an infinite number of ways to teach children how to read, for instance. Schools, if they are to survive, must meet the learning needs of children, or families will vote with their feet. In the end, what makes a good school are good teachers, helping children learn. Without this interaction, the educational process can become quite hollow.

Choice schools can be oases of authenticity, genuine learning environments, as we have seen in some of the case studies in chapter 2. This does not mean that school choice automatically leads to better schools. It does mean that choice may be one of the conditions that help to create an environment of innovation. If innovation is coupled with accountability, then we have created a policy matrix for schools that address the needs of children. From observation I would suggest that these child-centered schools can be characterized as fostering three elements: attachment, active knowledge, and self-reliance.

Human beings are intensely social animals. The development of the brain itself is related to participation in society (Persell and Cookson 1992). Countless studies demonstrate the importance of bonding for the development of human beings and other higher primates. Young chimpanzees, if they are deprived of mothering support, have their growth stunted and often die. Human babies who do not have reliable nurturing figures early in their lives also suffer developmentally and may die. As we have seen, in today's world many children are not able to successfully attach to their families. These children are at maximum risk. Child-centered schools increase the likelihood that children will be able to attach to nurturing figures. These schools should be small, warm, and consistent. Effective schools are warm schools, ineffective schools are indifferent schools, destructive schools are cold. Nothing will freeze the heart of a child faster than a cold family and a cold school.

Most educators also know that learning curves are highly related to the "use value" of knowledge. In order to draw out their innate learning capacities and creativities, children must identify with the material that is being taught. To be vital, knowledge must be active. Education, in the true sense, is always experiential because experience turns knowledge into action and behavior. This observation is particularly important in an era when knowledge itself is being transformed at a fantastic rate. The children we educate today will be living in a far different world than that of their parents or teachers. Survival and thrival for children require that their creativity and critical capacities be developed so as to maximize their intellectual flexibility, acuity, and capacity for growth. These characteristics of mind are not simply attractive adornments to learning; they are the core characteristics of an open and engaged mind. Without them our society's civic consciousness will become increasingly constricted and individuals will not be able to compete in the social and economic marketplace.

Last, children must learn to separate and become independent from their parents and from their schools. We live in a society that breeds dependencies. People are dependent upon others for their thinking. They often depend on chemistry to control their moods. And they often depend on mass entertainment for emotional substance. Just as autonomy is a key element in creating accountable schools, individuals have a need for autonomy if they are to live responsible and accountable lives. Conformity is the opposite of self-reliance, and schools that advocate conformity can create generations of students whose creative and intellectual potentials are stunted and sometimes destroyed. Schools that provide students with learning opportunities that promote autonomy and self-reliance are helping to strengthen the very fabric of democracy.

If managed school choice can create oases of authenticity and warmth in the very center of a cold and often hostile society, then it is a policy we cannot afford not to utilize. This is not to say that the only kinds of choice schools that provide real choice are progressive schools. Not every child does well in a relatively unstructured environment, and families are entitled to send their children to schools that reflect their own values. Choice may be a way of overcoming the inertia that characterizes large public school bureaucracies, especially in the inner city. To make choice more than a school-design addendum, we should give serious thought to restructuring American education and eliminating the structural inequalities that keep our society divided, stagnant, and prone to violence.

A New Educational Covenant

A justice-driven educational system requires that all children have an equal share of the community's educational resources; it also requires that we provide incentives to educational innovators to revitalize their schools while at the same time holding them accountable for their students' intellectual growth, physical safety, and moral development. I am suggesting a plan for the revitalization of public education that includes an educational trust fund for every American child, managed public school choice, and the creation of model schools. In the proposal detailed below, the rationale for these policy suggestions and a plan for their implementation are outlined. Obviously, some details related to such a plan cannot be included in a proposal, but I feel confident that its main elements provide a coherent direction for the transformation of American education. The underlying principle of the plan is that we must enter into a new educational covenant that gives high priority to the welfare of children, to the revitalization of the democratic vision, and to the celebration of learning.

This plan does not include private school choice in the strict sense because I believe that ultimately any large-scale voucher plan will undermine public education and lead to a form of educational anarchy. There is, however, one exception to this position. Within the inner city there are private schools, including religious schools, that deserve public support because they are educating disadvantaged students at a time when public-sector schools are in disarray. To let these private schools close because they lack funds could cause a great deal of harm to the children in the inner city. Traditionally, a high wall between church and state has kept the state from financing religious schools. The Supreme Court's current interpretation of the Constitution makes it virtually impossible for religious schools to receive more than very small amounts of public money. I believe that this position is too stringent. We ought to reconceptualize the constitutional issues related to the public funding of private schools by applying the "child-benefit theory" to issues of governmental support for religious organizations. In essence, the child-benefit theory balances the needs of children against the requirement that the state not establish a state religion. It seems clear to me that balancing the needs of the children in the inner city against a strict interpretation of the Constitution should result in a policy that allows the state to support schools that educate children who, if they did not attend these schools, would in all likelihood attend no schools at all.

The United States is perhaps the only country in the world where the separation of church and state is so firmly established by law and in public consciousness. This policy has served the United States well because it has reduced religious conflict. Creating a large-scale voucher system in which families could use public funds to send their children to private schools might have harmful effects, including the unintended encouragement of religious conflict and the establishment of fringe schools. Paradoxically, it might threaten the distinctiveness of private schools by making them more like public schools. How, therefore, can public-service private schools in the inner city be supported by public funds without opening the Pandora's box of private school vouchers?

On the basis of the child-benefit theory, I suggest that inner-city private schools which have student bodies composed of 60 percent or more of children whose families' incomes are at or below the poverty line be entitled to long-term low-interest educational loans from banks and other lending institutions, guaranteed by individual states and the federal government. Educational loans could be used by the schools to improve their facilities, to pay their staffs a living wage, and to promote their programs within the community. These loans would be available to both religious and nonreligious schools. Private schools that did not educate the disadvantaged would not be entitled. It is important to support institutions that serve the neediest children, regardless of their form of governance. By extending loans to inner-city private schools, a large-scale voucher plan is avoided while at the same time making resources available to institutions that deserve them. Part of a new educational covenant is a generosity of spirit and the willingness to put the lives of children before all else. We have a responsibility toward children regardless of their parents' financial status, racial characteristics, or beliefs. A significant measure of a good society is the degree to which it reveres its children. Thus, an alternative design for public education ought to begin with the basic educational and social goals of community trust, individual freedom, and collective responsibility.

A fundamental principle of this alternative educational design is that every child has the same right to educational opportunity as every other child. This does not mean that all children have equal talent, or that we should expect all children to reach the same level of academic proficiency.

The right of access refers to the social obligation of the community not to discriminate against a child because of family characteristics or personal limitations. Every child is entitled to an educational share. This share can be used at a public school of choice. In a society that is highly stratified and where the financing of education is also highly stratified, it is necessary in a redesign plan that the monetary worth of an educational share be in inverse relation to the family's income. The poorer the child, the greater his or her educational share. In effect, every child receives at birth an educational trust fund that guarantees equal access to the public schools of his or her choice. How these trust funds will be financed will be discussed in the proposal itself. The fundamental concept of the educational trust fund is that we, as a community, make a commitment to children that their life opportunities will not be foreshortened for reasons of their birth.

Experience with controlled choice has shown that managed public school choice can create racial integration, involve parents in the education of their children, and lay the groundwork for the rejuvenation of public schools. Interdistrict public school choice makes every public school a magnet school. Public schools in a managed choice system would continue to receive revenues raised through taxation and state-operated gambling. However, these revenues would cover only 70 percent of the school's operating budget. The remaining 30 percent would have to be raised by attracting poor students who have educational shares to spend. A public school that receives such educational shares from students must ensure that 20 percent of its student body is composed of those whose family's incomes are at or below the poverty line. It is important to remember that these students receive larger shares than others and are thus economically attractive. The key incentive for public schools to recruit share students, especially share students from disadvantaged homes, is that the schools retain any surplus accrued during the school year in order to improve their programs, reimburse their faculty, or maintain the school itself. This method of financing public education balances the need for a strong, publicly supported school system with the need to stimulate competition among public schools. Managed school choice is a method of encouraging schools to innovate by rewarding those schools with educational vision and social commitment.

Equity is a necessary but not a sufficient condition for a true educational transformation. Just as a community has the obligation to protect its children and to guarantee equal educational opportunity, so it also has the obligation to promote individual and family liberty. Thus, if teachers and parents are able to found schools that do not violate the conditions of the educational covenant discussed above, these may be designated "model schools" and made eligible to receive shares from children's educational trust funds. Model schools must have fifty or more students and must enroll at least 20 percent of their students from families whose incomes are at or below the poverty line. If the founders of model schools do not violate the rule of equal access, then the state should have only a small role to play in monitoring and regulating the schools.

The Proposal
The central purposes of this educational share plan are to promote educational experimentation, to provide equal access to educational opportunity for all American children, and to create a superior system of public schools in the United States.

The Educational Trust Fund
Who is entitled to shares in the educational trust fund?

1. Every native born American child has a right to shares in the educational trust fund. Each child's fund will be established one year after his or her birth.

2. Non-native-born children aged one year or more are entitled to a trust fund from the date of their first entrance into the American educational system.

How will the shares be distributed?

1. Every child must receive a social security number by his or her first birthday. An educational trust fund cannot be established until a child has acquired a social security number.

2. A computerized data base will be established for each one-year-old child and will be updated as needed. The data base will include name, date of birth, home address, and notation of any handicapping conditions.

3. Each child will receive an educational share from the Department of Education in the state in which he or she resides. State departments of education may lawfully appoint certain financial institutions to act as their agent for the distribution of shares.

4. The monetary worth of a share shall be determined by a formula that reflects the following principle: the lower the family income of a child, the greater the value of his or her share. Family income will be determined according to federal tax returns. If parents do not file an income tax return, their yearly income may be determined by alternate means.

5. At no time shall the monetary worth of a share exceed the annual average per pupil cost of education in the state where the child resides.

6. Shares will be sent to students' homes. If a student has no known address or is without a home, his or her share will be sent to the central office of the last school district in which the student was a resident.

7. Unclaimed shares will be sent to the central office of the last school district in which the student was known to reside. These shares will remain for three months in the school district and, if unclaimed, will be returned to the state Department of Education.

8. Shares cannot be accumulated from year to year, nor are they transferable between recipients.

9. All interest accruing from educational shares will revert to the state and not to the child or his or her family.

How will the educational shares be financed?

1. On the premise that the present method of financing public educa-

tion is unconstitutional because it denies students equal protection under the law, states will revise their current method of collecting property taxes as it relates to school finance. The purpose of this revision is to equalize the amount of money available for spending on education between and within school districts. (Recently, Kentucky passed a law that provided for equal financial support of the school districts in the state.)

2. Part of the revenues raised through property taxes will finance 40 percent of the educational trust funds. An additional 25 percent will be financed through other state forms of taxation, including the sales tax. Another 20 percent will be raised through public lotteries. The federal government will contribute 15 percent, either through a special bond issue or by budgetary allocations. Other revenues needed to support public-sector schools will be raised through property taxes, user taxes, and state-supported gambling.

3. All revenue will be kept in trust by the state departments of education or their fiduciary designees.

Managed Choice and Model Schools
What types of schools may receive educational shares?

1. All currently operating public schools may receive educational shares. Public schools will receive 70 percent of their revenues directly from the state departments of education, 30 percent of their revenues must be raised through educational shares. All public schools that receive educational shares must make a commitment to accept at least 20 percent of their students from disadvantaged backgrounds. Any monetary surplus a public school accumulates may be retained by that school for purposes of school improvement.

2. Newly founded model schools may also receive educational shares. These schools may be founded by teachers and parents in collaboration with other educational providers. A model school must have a population of at least fifty students and provisions for fiduciary respon-

sibility. Model schools may not espouse hatred or hostility toward others on the basis of race, ethnicity, social class, religion, handi-capping condition, or gender. Model schools must also meet the requirement of equal educational access. All model schools must make a commitment to accept at least 20 percent of their students from disadvantaged backgrounds.

4. Model schools may set whatever admissions criteria they wish as long as these criteria do not discriminate against students in terms of race, ethnicity, class, or gender. Schools that do not admit students with handicaps may have limits set on the amount of educational shares they may receive.

5. All model schools will be subject to state requirements concerning health, safety, and student welfare. The state reserves the right to close a school if it violates standards of health, safety, and student welfare.

6. All schools that are eligible to receive educational shares must fully disclose publicly their missions, their tables of organization, their curricula, and such pertinent financial information as may be required by the state. This information will be made available to parents and children through published reports distributed through parent information centers.

7. Every model school must be insured and bonded to protect consumers from fraud, incompetence, and malfeasance.

Issues of Implementation

This proposal is meant to provide a conceptual framework upon which individual state plans could be developed, although the essential components could not be substantially changed without weakening the entire structure. To my mind there are three major areas of concern in terms of implementing this proposal: the distribution of the educational shares, consumer information, and consumer protection.

The Distribution of the Educational Shares

Clearly, one of the primary requirements for the transformation of American education is ending bureaucratic control over individual schools. Part of the reason that state and city educational bureaucracies have grown in the past forty-five years is that they have taken on a wide variety of functions. Some of these functions are directly related to teaching and learning, but many are related to the maintenance of the bureaucracies themselves. This has proved to be an obstacle to genuine educational reform. It would make little sense to dismantle the bureaucratic regulation of schools only to substitute another bureaucracy to distribute educational shares. The role of the state in the regulation of education and in the distribution of educational shares should be minimal.

The responsibilities of the state unit that would administer educational trust funds are to be extremely circumscribed. These responsibilities would include: (1) to collect and "bank" the trust funds from the four sources of income mentioned earlier; (2) to collect the names, addresses, levels of family income, and information about possible handicapping conditions of all students who have received a social security number and are state residents; (3) to determine the value of each child's educational share according to the formula determined by the state legislature; and (4) to create the shares and distribute them. In states with populations over ten million, many of these tasks could be divided into geographical subsections in order to reduce the error and delay often associated with organizations servicing a large number of clients.

Before the advent of the computer, the distribution of educational shares might have been cumbersome; sophisticated computer systems, however, have made large-scale data processing feasible. Undoubtedly, for children who come from highly transient families or from families without homes, there would be difficulties related to administering the share system. Yet, the use of computerized data bases will prevent children from being lost in the system as long as each child has a social security number. If a child seeks enrollment in a school district other than that in which he or she has originally enrolled, a computerized data search will reveal the size of the child's share. When families relocate across state lines, they may apply for a new share. Students who transfer during the school year will have the value of their share determined on a pro rata basis. Many possible efficiencies can be built into such a system. In any case, because the authority of the units administering the educational trust funds is focused and limited, it will be relatively easy for outside auditors to evaluate their operations.

Parent Information Centers

School choice and social trust are contingent upon accessible and accurate information. One of the main benefits of encouraging student and parental choice is that it compels schools to identify their missions, examine their strengths and weaknesses, and make this information available to families. Research in parent information centers indicates that a critical element in ensuring that parents and children use the centers fully is an intense effort by those who manage the centers to reach every family in the community, through mailings, radio and television announcements, posters, and visits to churches, nursery schools, laundromats, shopping centers, and other locales where families are likely to gather. Information should be made available in the languages of the children living in the community. Moreover, parent information centers should treat each family as unique and dignify the process by which families choose schools. Information collected at the centers can be used to supplement other information the state may need in order to determine the residences of children. In essence, parent information centers are community resources that bring schools and families together and act as benign brokers of educational choice. Without investments in these centers, the process of school choice becomes chaotic, uninformed, and potentially destructive to children.

Consumer Protection

Advocates of free-market choice sometimes fail to recognize that fraudulent marketing in education can deprive children of the education to which they are entitled. Moreover, it is the responsibility of the state to ensure that taxpayer dollars are not wasted through fraud or incompetence. It is extremely important that educational trust funds be used to support legitimate enterprises that fulfill the educational promises they make. It is essential that every public and model school that accepts educational shares report annually to the state on its educational mission, organizational framework, the characteristics of its faculty and students, and its financial condition. It is also important that the state reserve the right to investigate complaints by visiting schools and subpoenaing relevant records. Serious complaints of fraudulent practices could be channeled through consumer protection officers working in parent information centers. These officers could turn their findings over to the local district attorney's office if they deemed that a case warranted further investigation. Parents who wish to educate their children at home may not receive educational shares because there is no reasonable way to monitor whether the shares are used for childrens' education.

No School Is an Island

America needs a vibrant, strong, and democratic public school system. There is also a need to reinvent the public school system so that it meets the needs of children and families. School choice is a tactic for reform, but not an overall strategy. Without resources, purpose, and commitment, American public education will continue to wither and perhaps die. The debate over school choice is in some ways a metaphor of what constitutes not only the good school but the good society. Much of this debate has been unproductive because it has ignored the real world of schools, families, and children. I believe that choice can be a mechanism for achieving a school system that is just, innovative, and academically productive. It is a method by which we can reinvent public education, reintegrate schools into their communities, and redefine community. Schools can become oases of authenticity in a troubled and often alienating world. We might ask ourselves what we hope for our children, for our children's children, and for their children in the next century. Is it a world that is ecologically depleted, ripped apart by ethnic and racial hatred, a world where the poor and the rich are divided and antagonistic? Under these conditions democracy cannot long survive. A strong public school system is the nursery of democracy. It is the obligation of the present generation to create the conditions where children and young people can develop intellectually, physically, aesthetically, and morally. We need to keep reinventing democracy and to keep the ideals of equality and liberty alive.

Appendix   School-Choice Legislative Activity across the Nation

Alabama

Alabama has a voluntary intradistrict controlled-choice program that was adopted into law by the state legislature in 1991. Districts and schools may choose whether to establish or participate in choice programs; their policies for transferring and accepting students must comply with guidelines for promoting and maintaining racial and ethnic balance. The current plan, which is intrasectional, includes no provision for tax credits or vouchers. During the 1991 legislative session, a bill was introduced and defeated that would have established a system of statewide public and private choice for Alabama parents and students. The proposed plan also would have set up a state aid system whereby education funds would follow the student to the school of his or her choice.

Alaska

There are no existing choice programs in Alaska, nor any legislation pending that would define or formally establish a system of parental choice. Gov. Walter Hickel's (I) choice task force report was released in March 1992. The report was commissioned to investigate choice and other school reform issues supporting the establishment of a charter schools program, but it does not call for any reform programs that would include mandatory choice at this time.

Arizona

Arizona, like many states, has traditionally had an informal system of interdistrict school choice; there are currently no legislated or mandated programs in effect. A task force on education organized by Gov. Fyfe Symington (R) has been actively involved in educational reform and supports choice as an integral part of its plans for improving Arizona's schools. The task forces's recommendations on choice were introduced as legislation during the 1991 session; the cohesive choice plan included mandatory interdistrict open enrollment, charter schools, vouchers, and intersectional choice. This legislation did not pass. However, support for the measure remains strong.

Arkansas

Arkansas has a system of statewide voluntary, interdistrict open enrollment. Choice is viewed as a one strategy of many that can be used to increase the effectiveness of education and schools. It was adopted as part of a 1989 school reform initiative that was passed by the state legislature. During the 1990–91 school year, close to one-third of all districts participated in choice. Providing parents with ample information about schools and the choice program in general is an important part of Arkansas' choice plan; so is the state's commitment to funding transportation of students between districts. There are no provisions for vouchers or tax credits in the program.

California

California's current school choice program is informal and voluntary. It is supported by existing provisions in the state education code that allow students to attend school in districts other than their own. Districts can create intra- or interdistrict choice programs at their own discretion and without any supervision or control by the state board. Because of this, choice in California is not formally tracked or even labeled as "choice." Only one district, the Richmond Unified School District, has a formally labeled and publicized plan. During the 1991 state legislative session, a wide variety of bills were drafted and introduced to establish choice as an educational policy. All but one of these plans, ranging from basic intradistrict to statewide open enrollment to intersectional (private and public choice), were defeated. Discussion of the one remaining bill, which would streamline and extend interdistrict choice to a statewide scale, was left open at the end of the 1991 legislature. Charter school legislation was approved by the Senate on June 4, 1992. Under the terms of SB 1448, California could have up to one hundred charter schools (no more than ten per district). EXCEL (Excellence through Choice in Education League) filed a voucher proposal late in 1991 that would institute a full-scale voucher system for all schoolchildren of California. As of Aug. 22, 1992, this voucher proposal has been certified and has qualified for the June 1994 California ballot.

Colorado
Choice in Colorado is being developed within the context of a pilot program that is designed to implement school choice throughout the state on a limited, experimental level. The program, which is funded for five school years, provides for the creation of three intrasectional, interdistrict choice programs per year, one each in the Denver, Eastern Slope, and Western Slope areas. Colorado also offers a post-secondary options program involving high schools and colleges around the state.

Connecticut
Connecticut has no formal school choice plans, and no current legislation would support such a system. On March 13, 1992, the Education Committee of the Connecticut Assembly held a hearing on AB 323, which contains the Charter Schools Task Force findings regarding charter schools. The task force recommended the establishment of six charter schools in the state on a pilot basis, beginning in 1994.

Delaware
Delaware does not have any school choice programs, and no pending legislation seeks to establish choice plans. However, individual school districts may apply directly to the federal government for funds to implement locally developed choice programs.

District of Columbia
There are no school choice programs in the District, and no plans are currently being considered.

Florida

Currently, there are no mandated choice programs in Florida. Informal choice does exist in many districts throughout the state, in many different, locally developed forms. All of these plans are intrasectional and do not involve vouchers or tax credits. Additionally, Florida has an established system of magnet schools, alternative schools, and postsecondary options to serve the needs of its students. During the 1991 legislative session, a number of bills that addressed the choice issue were introduced. None passed. One of these bills supported public-private choice and the use of vouchers to increase the educational options available to low-income students. Although some support for these kinds of programs remains, no new legislation has been introduced.

Georgia

There are no choice programs in Georgia at this time.

Hawaii

Hawaii, consisting of a single school district, does not have a school choice system. Legislation was introduced during the 1991 session that would enable students to transfer between any schools in-state, but the proposal has not yet been passed.

Idaho

In 1990 Idaho enacted a plan for voluntary statewide open enrollment. The plan, which began during the 1991–92 school year, is intrasectional and therefore does not involve any use of vouchers. Education aid dollars follow the student to the school of his or her choice; the receiving district is reimbursed through state-issued tuition certificates. The Idaho choice program does not provide funding for transporting students between districts, nor does it include any formal system of informing parents about potential choices or schools. As of this time, no further choice legislation is pending.

Illinois

No formalized system of choice is currently in place in Illinois, although informal choice is a component of many districts in the state. In 1991 the state Board of Education commissioned a task force to investigate policy options and to explore any potential interest in choice. There was little support for vouchers or for including nonpublic schools in the range of choices available to parents. During the 1990 term a bill that would have created a voucher system failed to pass, and the 1991 session saw a variety of choice bills introduced and defeated. No further legislation is pending.

Indiana
A bill sponsored by senators Morris Mills and Lewis Mahern was introduced in 1992. It would "provide scholarships for all children in the state to use at any school of their choice, reduce regulation of scholarship-redeeming schools and give teachers and schools more autonomy, provide for statewide testing, and add new measures to help preschool children." As of mid-1993, the bill had not been brought to the Senate floor

Iowa
In 1989 Iowa adopted legislation that established a trial program of statewide inter-district open enrollment. This choice policy was later made mandatory, beginning in the 1990–91 school year. Also part of the state choice program is a system of postsecondary options for high-school students. Iowa provides assistance for the interdistrict transportation of students through vouchers. It also issues tax credits for parents of students who attend nonpublic schools. Local districts are responsible for providing information about schools and choices to parents; there is no statewide information program. No further legislation concerning choice is pending.

Kansas
There are no formal choice programs in Kansas at this time. During the 1991 legislative session, one bill was introduced that supported the establishment of intersectional choice for students in the Wichita school district; no action on this proposal has yet been taken. A statewide voucher bill entitled "G.I. Bill for Children" was proposed in 1992 by Sen. Eric Yost. No further action regarding this bill had been taken as of mid-1993.

Kentucky
Kentucky has no formal choice programs. However, in the landmark 1990 legal decision that declared Kentucky's school finance system unconstitutional and

many of its schools unsatisfactory, the state Supreme Court called for a top-to-bottom reform of the state's schools and school funding. Included in the reform package was a provision for students to attend a private school at state expense if it was determined that their public school would provide an unfair or inadequate education.

Louisiana

No formal choice or open-enrollment programs currently exist in Louisiana. Legislation introduced during the 1991 session would have gradually phased in a system of intersectional, voucher-based choice, but the bill was defeated. The state Board of Education does not support a choice movement, and no additional bills are pending.

Maine

Maine does not have any formal choice programs, although students living in isolated communities are allowed to attend schools in districts other than their own. An open-enrollment bill backed by Gov. John McKernan (R) was introduced during the 1991 legislative session, but it never passed out of the Education Committee of the lower house.

Maryland

No choice programs currently exist in Maryland. A bill introduced in the legislature in 1991 would have supported choice for low-income students in the Baltimore area, but it failed to pass. The state Board of Education does not endorse the idea of choice or any move to legally establish such a system; however, a number of bills pending in the legislature support the implementation of choice.

Massachusetts

A law passed in 1991 permits voluntary intrasectional choice; each district may determine how and if it will participate in choice. A district may join an inter-district program, create its own intradistrict open-enrollment system, or choose not to formally engage in choice at all. Every Massachusetts student has the right and opportunity to attend the school of his or her choice, although acceptance by a school or district depends on promoting and maintaining a racial balance. State aid dollars follow students to the school they attend, although there is no state subsidy for transporting students between districts. Prominent choice plans exist in such districts as Cambridge and Boston. No further legislation concerning choice is pending.

Michigan

Two choice bills were passed by the Michigan legislature in 1991. The first set the stage for districts to develop a system of voluntary intradistrict open enrollment. The second allocated funds to start interdistrict pilot programs. Both went into effect in September 1992, and both choice plans are supported by the state Board of Education. No additional legislation concerning choice is pending.

Minnesota

Minnesota has a long history of promoting choice in its education system; in 1983 the state adopted a pilot program for developing the choice programs that exist, by law, today. In 1988 the legislature established a system of intrasectional, statewide, intra- and interdistrict open enrollment; the program became mandatory in 1990–91. Minnesota subsidizes the transportation of students between districts and supports a network that gives parents information about school choice options for their children. Tax credits are available to the parents of children who attend nonpublic schools. Minnesota was the first state to set up a system of postsecondary options and second-chance programs, which today are fully integrated into the spectrum of choices available to students and parents. In 1991 the Minnesota legislature passed the Charter Schools Act, which established a context for teachers to create and run innovative schools apart from traditional bureaucratic and administrative structures. It is hoped that these new public schools will increase the range of choices for public school parents and students. No further choice legislation is pending.

Mississippi

There are no formal choice programs in Mississippi. Legislation that would have established a choice plan was defeated in 1989; no further legislative action has been taken.

Missouri

Missouri does not have a legislated or state-supported choice plan in effect. Kansas City and St. Louis, however, have magnet school systems that involve the transfer of students between urban and suburban districts. These programs were developed as a strategy to promote desegregation goals in these urban areas; they are not duplicated elsewhere in the state. Legislation to establish mandatory statewide choice was defeated in 1989 and 1990. In 1991 a ballot initiative calling for mandatory statewide choice was defeated by popular vote. No further choice legislation is pending.

Montana

There are no choice programs in Montana; legislation that sought to develop such a program was defeated in 1990 and no further bills have been introduced.

Nebraska

Nebraska passed a plan for voluntary statewide, intrasectional open enrollment in 1989, and the legislature adopted additional measures in 1990 and 1991. The 1991 "emergency" school reform act provided for the immediate implementation of choice on a statewide level. Districts in Nebraska may participate in both intra- and interdistrict programs; a student may attend any school in the state and must, within guidelines, be accepted. The state Board of Education provides funding for the interdistrict transport of low-income students. Nebraska's open enrollment will gradually expand to include all districts, and by the 1993–94 school year, choice will be mandatory for all districts in the state.

Nevada

Nevada does not have a system of choice. A bill that sought to establish choice was defeated in 1989.

New Hampshire

There are no formally sanctioned choice programs in New Hampshire, although many local districts have developed and participate in informal choice arrangements. Legislation that would have imposed a statewide system of open enrollment was defeated in 1990 and again in 1991. New Hampshire also has a tax credit program for the parents of children who attend nonpublic schools. There are no bills that would establish a system of statewide choice currently in the state legislature.

New Jersey

New Jersey does not have a formally supported system of choice. Informal intradistrict choice programs do exist in some New Jersey districts, generally involving the use of magnet schools. Existing state law permits interdistrict choice, based on the discretion of the potential receiving district; state aid may or may not follow the student, depending on individual circumstances. In 1992 Assembly Democratic leader Joseph Doria introduced a school choice bill that includes a statewide interdistrict open-enrollment program and a voucher-type program that includes nonpublic schools.

New Mexico

There are no legislated choice programs in New Mexico; legislation that would have created a statewide system was defeated in 1989. Only the urban Santa Fe district has an open-enrollment program.

New York

New York has no formally established choice or open-enrollment programs, although many districts throughout the state successfully allow parents and students to make informal intrasectional school choices. New York City, for example, has an extensive network of magnet high schools. These schools, some with strict admissions requirements, offer specialized vocational and academic programs, to which any student in the city may apply. The city is also the home of District 4, located in a low-income neighborhood on Manhattan's East Side. The district's innovative use of public school choice, within a larger context of school restructuring and reform, is an effective strategy to combat the educational hazards of inner-city schools. In 1991 the New York state Board of Regents defeated a proposal that sought to create an intersectional voucher system for low-income students who live in neighborhoods with "substandard" schools. The plan would have allowed parents to redeem their vouchers at a public or private school other than the one regularly assigned. Choice is not an active political issue in New York, and the state Board of Education does not support legislative approaches to developing choice programs. The state legislature held hearings on the choice issue in 1989, but no bills were introduced as a result; since that time, no further legislation has been considered.

North Carolina

Currently, no choice programs exist in North Carolina. In 1989 and again in 1991 the state legislature held preliminary hearings about the choice issue, but neither round of discussions prompted the introduction of a bill. Additionally, bills that would have supported public school choice died in committee in both 1990 and 1991. No further legislation had been introduced as of mid-1993.

North Dakota

North Dakota does not have any choice programs. There was no choice legislation pending or legislative activity on the subject as of mid-1993.

Ohio

In 1989 the Ohio legislature enacted a statewide, intrasectional open-enrollment law. The plan, which was refined in 1991, established a system of voluntary intra- and interdistrict choice. Over the next few years, intradistrict choice will be expanded and will be mandatory by the 1993–94 school year; interdistrict choice will continue to be voluntary. So far, district participation in both forms of choice has been extremely limited. The state subsidizes the transportation costs of students who choose to transfer between districts, and state aid dollars follow the student to the district in which he or she attends school. Ohio also has a postsecondary options program in place. No further legislation on the subject of choice has been introduced.

Oklahoma

Oklahoma does not have any formal choice programs. There has, however, been some recent legislative activity. Choice legislation was introduced, but killed, in 1989 and 1990; new choice proposals were discussed during the 1991 session, but they never left the Education Committee. An educational reform act, passed in May 1991, created a six-member "deregulation committee" to study the feasibility of loosening the existing education laws governing the interdistrict transfer of students. The idea of a flexible transfer rule was cited as a crucial component of school reform, although there were no direct references to choice.

Oregon

In 1991 the Oregon legislature passed a plan that established a voluntary system of inter- and intrasectional public school open enrollment. Although the system is theoretically statewide and universal, in practice its use is fairly limited. Both of the bill's provisions require a student to meet specific guidelines before he or she may transfer between schools or districts. The first provision allows students who are performing below grade level in their assigned school to attend another school of their choice, provided it will accept them; the second provision sets up an extensive program of vocational and academic postsecondary options for all students who have completed tenth grade and received a basic skills certificate. In the November 1990 general election voters defeated a ballot initiative that would have provided a $2,500 voucher/tax credit to parents who sent their children to private schools or supported a home-schooling program.

Pennsylvania

No formal programs of choice exist in Pennsylvania, although there is significant popular support for the development of a legally sanctioned choice system. A 1990 bill that would have funded $900 scholarship grants, available to all parents and redeemable at public or private schools, was passed by the state Senate but defeated by the House. No new legislation has been formally introduced, although the grant proposal and other choice measures may be reintroduced in the near future.

Rhode Island

Rhode Island does not have a formally established choice system, and there has never been any legislative activity on the subject. In 1989 the state Board of Education created a commission to study including choice in a school reform plan; the report, issued in the fall of 1989, outlined plans for an informal pilot program that would support district proposals to create intradistrict controlled-choice programs. However, only two districts submitted plans and neither was implemented. The board does not back a legal approach to developing choice. Interestingly, an April 1991 survey found that informal choice structures actually did exist in districts across the state.

South Carolina

South Carolina has no open-enrollment programs. No choice legislation is pending, although some discussion of choice issues is currently taking place in the legislature's Education Committee. During the 1991 session, two open-enrollment bills were introduced, but no action was taken on either. The South Carolina Board of Education supports the development of locally initiated choice efforts, but it does not sanction a legal approach to the subject. In 1992 two bills expanding the availability of home schooling to parents were signed into law.

South Dakota

There are no choice programs in South Dakota. No legislation was pending as of mid-1993.

Tennessee

Although no legislated choice programs exist in Tennessee, an extensive system of informal intra- and interdistrict open enrollment exists. A 1925 state law allows districts to accept students from other districts, with state aid following the child to his or her chosen district and school. In 1991 the legislature defeated a bill that would have created an intersectional voucher plan. No further legislation has been proposed, although there seems to be political and popular support for an intersectional approach to choice. In 1992 a charter school proposal was presented and referred to committee for further study.

Texas

There are no official choice programs in Texas, although existing state law permits interdistrict transfers. A 1989–90 study by a state Board of Education committee found that a few districts, including Houston, have working intradistrict open-enrollment plans, often as part of a strategy to meet desegregation goals. A 1991 bill sought to create an intersectional voucher system for low-income students in fourteen districts, but it did not pass out of the House Education Committee. No further legislation has been proposed. In 1992 a group of CEOs in San Antonio announced the CEO Foundation, initially funded at $1.5 million to pay up to $750 per student for over seven hundred low-income students to attend a public or private school of their choice.

Utah

In 1990 the Utah legislature passed a plan that established a formal program of voluntary statewide, intrasectional open enrollment. Previously, intradistrict choice plans have existed in many districts around the state, many based on magnet schools; some districts participated in interdistrict transfers. The 1990 legislation formalizes these practices and provides that 50 percent of the state education aid for each child follows the student to the school and district he or she chooses; the remainder of the funds is divided between the sending and receiving districts. There is no state subsidy for interdistrict transportation. So far, there has been limited participation in the new programs.

Vermont

Vermont does not have a formal system of school choice, and no pending legislation would establish such a system. However, Vermont has had an informal voucher system in place since 1894. Because of the rural nature of the state, many communities do not operate schools; in these cases, they may issue tuition vouchers backed by local funds that are redeemable at almost any public or private school. Exceptions include a 1961 law that prohibits these vouchers from being used at parochial schools and a provision for communities to restrict the private schools where their vouchers are eligible.

Virginia

Virginia does not have a system of school choice. A bill supporting open enrollment within a district was considered in 1993.

Washington

In 1990 the Washington legislature passed a statewide choice plan. Called "Learning by Choice," it set up a system of voluntary intradistrict open enrollment and mandatory interdistrict choice, although the plan restricts the use of interdistrict transfers. Interdistrict choice is encouraged, but a district may impose restrictions on admission. The state provides a subsidy for the interdistrict transportation of students, but there is no state-coordinated system of informing parents of their potential choices. Bills that seek to implement an intersectional voucher program for low-income students were introduced near the end of the 1991 legislative session, but as of mid-1993 no action had been taken.

West Virginia

West Virginia does not support any formal choice programs. A bill that would have created a system of public school open enrollment was defeated in 1991. During the 1992 session, two pieces of legislation were introduced. One would create a tax credit program for parents who send their children to private schools or who teach their children at home. The other would set up a pilot voucher program. No action has yet been taken on either plan.

Wisconsin

Wisconsin does not have a system of statewide open enrollment; legislation that would have created such a program was defeated in 1989. In 1990 the state legislature passed the Milwaukee Parental Choice Law, which set up a limited intersectional voucher plan for the Milwaukee school district. The plan provides vouchers, worth $2,500, to a thousand low-income students; the vouchers may be redeemed at any public or participating nonsectarian private school in Milwaukee. This plan has caused widespread controversy and sustained repeated challenges to its constitutionality. However, the Wisconsin Supreme Court recently declared the plan constitutional and fully in line with the state education code. To date, there has not been any legislative activity to expand the program elsewhere in the state, although Gov. Tommy Thompson (R) supports such a plan. The state Board of Education opposes this system on the grounds that the use of vouchers is equivalent to direct state aid to private schools, at the expense of the public school system.

Wyoming

There are no formal open-enrollment programs in Wyoming, although an informal interdistrict transfer system, where state aid dollars follow students to their chosen district and school, has traditionally operated throughout the state. No legislation to implement further choice structures was pending as of mid-1993.

References

Adler, Mortimer. 1982. *The Paideia Proposal*. New York: Macmillan.

Alexander, Karl, and Aaron Pallas. 1983. "Private Schools and Public Policy: New Evidence on Cognitive Achievement in Public and Private Schools." *Sociology of Education* 56: 170–82.

Allis, Sam. 1991, May 27. "Can Catholic Schools Do It Better?" *Time*, 48–49.

Alvarado, Anthony J. 1991, April 30. "Beyond Buzzwords in Education." *New York Times*, A19.

Alves, Michael J., and Charles V. Willie. 1987. "Controlled Choice Assignment: A New and More Effective Approach to School Desegregation." *Urban Review* 19(2): 67–87.

———. 1990. "Choice, Decentralization and Desegregation: The Boston 'Controlled Choice' Plan." In William H. Clune and John F. Witte, eds., *Choice and Control in American Education. Vol. 2: The Practice of Choice, Decentralization and School Restructuring* (pp. 17–75). New York: Falmer.

Archer, Margaret S. 1979. *Social Origins of Educational Systems*. London: Sage.

Arons, Stephen. 1983. *Compelling Belief: The Culture of American Schooling*. New York: McGraw-Hill.

Bauch, Patricia A. 1989. "Can Poor Parents Make Wise Educational Choices?" In William L. Boyd and James G. Cibulka, eds., *Private Schools and Public Policy: International Perspectives* (pp. 285–313). New York: Falmer.

Bellah, Robert N., et al. 1987. *Individualism and Commitment in American Life*. New York: Harper and Row.

Berg, Ivar E. 1971. *Education and Jobs: The Great Training Robbery*. Boston: Beacon.

Berger, Joseph. 1992a, Sept. 16. "Fernandez to Let Students Transfer to Any District." *New York Times*, A1, B4.

———. 1992b, Sept. 17. "Making School Choice Real Choice." *New York Times*, B1, B3.

Blank, Rolf K. 1989. *Educational Effects of Magnet Schools*. Madison: University of Wisconsin, National Center in Effective Secondary Schools, Wisconsin Center for Educational Research.

Blodgett, Bonnie. 1992, April. "The Private Hell of Public Education." *Lears*, 49–55.

Bolick, Clint. 1992. "Civil Rights and Parental Choice." Unpublished paper.

Bourdieu, Pierre, and Jean-Claude Passeron. 1977. *Reproduction: In Education, Society and Culture*. Beverly Hills, Calif.: Sage.

Bowles, Samuel, and Herbert Gintis. 1976. *Schooling in Capitalist America*. New York: Basic Books.

Boyer, Ernest. 1983. *High School*. New York: Harper and Row.

Bridge, R.G., and J. Blackman. 1978. *Family Choice in American Education: A Study of Alternatives in American Education*. Vol. 4. Santa Monica: Rand Corp.

Brown, Frank. 1992. "The Dutch Experience with School Choice: Implications for American Education." In Peter W. Cookson, Jr., ed., *The Choice Controversy* (pp. 171–89). Newbury Park, Calif.: Corwin.

Bush, George. 1992. "Remarks by the President in Ceremony for G.I. Bill Opportunity Scholarships for Children." White House press release.

Business/Higher Education Forum. 1983. *America's Competitive Challenge.* Washington, D.C.: American Council on Education.

Capell, F., Jr. 1978. A *Study in Alternatives in American Education.* Vol. 6: *Student Outcomes in Alum Rock, 1974–1976.* Santa Monica: Rand Corp.

Carnegie Foundation for the Advancement of Teaching. 1992. *School Choice.* Princeton, N.J..: Carnegie Foundation.

Carnegie Task Force on Teaching as a Profession. 1986. *A Nation Prepared: Teachers for the Twenty-first Century.* Washington, D.C.: Carnegie Forum on Education and the Economy.

Chubb, John E., and Terry M. Moe. 1990. *Politics, Markets, and America's Schools.* Washington, D.C.: Brookings Institution.

Clune, William H. 1990. "Educational Governance and Student Achievement." In William H. Clune and John F. Witte, eds., *Choice and Control in American Education.* Vol. 2: *The Practice of Choice, Decentralization and School Restructuring* (pp. 391–423). New York: Falmer.

Coleman, James S. 1992. "Some Points on Choice in Education." *Sociology of Education* 65(4): 260–62.

Coleman, James S., et al. 1966. *Equality of Opportunity.* Washington, D.C.: U.S. Government Printing Office.

Coleman, James S., and Thomas Hoffer. 1987. *Public and Private High Schools: The Impact of Communities.* New York: Basic Books.

Coleman, James S., Thomas Hoffer, and Sally Kilgore. 1982. *High School Achievement: Public, Catholic, and Private Schools Compared.* New York: Basic Books.

Coleman, James S., Kathryn Schiller, and Barbara Schneider. 1991. "Parental Involvement and School Choice." In *Resources and Actions: Parents, Their Children and Schools.* Chicago: NORC/University of Chicago Press.

Collins, Randall. 1971. "Functional and Conflict Theories of Educational Stratification." *American Sociological Review* 36: 1002–19.

Cookson, Peter W., Jr. 1981. "Private Secondary Boarding School and Public Suburban High School Graduation: An Analysis of College Attendance Plans." Ph.D. diss., New York University.

———. 1987a. "Closing the Rift between Scholarship and Practice: The Need to Revitalize Educational Research." *Educational Policy* 1: 321–31.

———. 1987b. "More, Different, or Better? Strategies for the Study of Private Education." *Educational Policy* 1: 289–94.

———. 1989. "United States of America: Contours of Continuity and Controversy in Private Schools." In Geoffrey Walford, ed., *Private Schools in Ten Countries* (pp. 57–84). New York: Routledge.

———. 1991a. "Private Schooling and Equity: Dilemmas of Choice." *Education and Urban Society* 23(2): 185–99.

———. 1991b. "Politics, Markets, and America's Schools: A Review." *Teachers College Record* 93: 156–60.

———. 1991c. "When Is a Little a Lot? Student Achievement, School Choice, and the Politics of Educational Research." Unpublished paper.

———. 1992. "The Ideology of Consumership and the Coming Deregulation of the Public School System." In Peter W. Cookson, Jr., ed., *The Choice Controversy* (pp. 83–99). Newbury, Calif.: Corwin.

Cookson, Peter W., Jr., and Caroline Hodges Persell. 1985. *Preparing for Power: America's Boarding Schools*. New York: Basic Books.

Cookson, Peter W., Jr., Alan R. Sadovnik, and Susan F. Semel. 1992. *International Handbook of Educational Reform*. New York: Greenwood.

Coombs, Philip H. 1985. *The World Crisis in Education: The View from the Eighties*. New York: Oxford University Press.

Coons, John E. 1992. "School Choice as Simple Justice." *First Things*, 15–22.

Coons, John E., and Stephen D. Sugarman. 1992. *Scholarships for Children*. Berkeley, Calif.: Institute of Governmental Studies Press.

Crain, Robert. 1992. "What Can New York City's Career Magnet High Schools Tell Us about the Choice Debate?" Paper delivered at "Choice: What Role in American Education?" Sponsored by the Economic Policy Institute, Washington, D.C.

Diegmueller, Karen. 1992, Jan. 8. "Despite Defeat, Choice Bill Likely to Resurface in PA." *Education Week*, 31.

Domanico, Raymond. 1989. *Model for Choice: A Report on Manhattan's District 4*. New York: Manhattan Institute Center for Educational Innovation.

———. 1990. *Restructuring New York City's Public Schools: The Case for Public School Choice*. New York: Manhattan Institute Center for Educational Innovation.

———. 1991. *A Model Public School Choice Plan for New York City School Districts*. New York: Manhattan Institute Center for Educational Innovation.

Dougherty, Kevin, and Lizabeth Sostre. 1992. "Minerva and the Market: The Sources of the Movement for School Choice." *Educational Policy* 6(2): 160–79.

Driscoll, Mary E. 1992. "Changing Minds and Changing Hearts: Choice, Achievement and School Community." Paper delivered at "Choice: What Role in American Education?" Sponsored by the Economic Policy Institute, Washington, D.C.

Education Commission of the United States. 1983. *Action for Excellence*. Boulder, Colo.: The Commission.

Edwards, T., J. Fritz, and G. Whitty. 1989. *The State and Private Education: An Evaluation of the Assisted Places Scheme*. London: Falmer.

Elam, Stanley M. 1990. "Trends in Support for Parental Choice." *Phi Delta Kappan* (September):43–44.

Elmore, Richard F. 1986. *Choice in Public Education*. Santa Monica, Calif.: Rand Corp.

———. 1990. "Choice as an Instrument of Public Policy: Evidence from Education and Health Care." In William H. Clune and John F. Witte, eds., *Choice and Control in American Education*. Vol. 1: *The Theory of Choice and Control in American Education* (pp. 285–317). New York: Falmer.

Erickson, Donald A. 1986. "Choice and Private Schools: Dynamics of Supply and Demand." In Daniel C. Levy, ed., *Private Education: Studies in Choice and Public Policy* (pp. 82–109). New York: Oxford University Press.

Everhart, Robert B. 1982. *The Public School Monopoly: A Critical Analysis of Education and State in American Society*. San Francisco: Pacific Institute.

Fitz, J., T. Edwards, and G. Whitty. 1986. "Beneficiaries, Benefits, and Costs: An Investigation of the Assisted Places Scheme." *Research Papers in Education* 1(3): 169–93.

Fliegel, Seymour. 1990. "Creative Non-Compliance." In William H. Clune and John F. Witte, eds., *Choice and Control in American Education*. Vol. 2: *The Practice of Choice, Decentralization and School Restructuring* (pp. 199–216). New York: Falmer.

Fowler, Frances C. 1992. "School Choice Policy in France: Success and Limitations." *Educational Policy* 6(4): 429–43.

Friedman, Milton. 1962. *Capitalism and Freedom*. Chicago: University of Chicago Press.

Gaw, Jonathan. 1991, July 28. "Vouchers an Rx for Pupils." *Los Angeles Times*, A3, A29.

Gibbs, Nancy. 1990, Oct. 8. "Shameful Bequests to the Next Generation." *Time*, 42–46.

Glenn, Charles L. 1989. *Choice of Schools in Six Nations*. Washington, D.C.: U.S. Government Printing Office.

————. 1991, January. "Why Are They So Afraid of School Choice?" Unpublished manuscript.

Goldberger, A. S., and G. G. Cain. 1982. "The Casual Analysis of Cognitive Outcomes in the Coleman, Hoffer and Kilgore Report." *Sociology of Education* 55: 103–22.

Goodlad, John. 1984. *A Place Called School*. New York: McGraw-Hill.

Harrington, Diane, and Peter W. Cookson, Jr. 1992. "School Reform in East Harlem: Alternative Schools vs. 'Schools of Choice.'" In G. Alfred Hess, ed., *Empowering Teachers and Parents: School Restructuring through the Eyes of Anthropologists* (pp. 177–86). Westport, Conn.: Bergin and Garvey.

Harrington, Michael. 1962. *The Other America*. New York: Macmillan.

Hess, G. Alfred, Jr. 1992. "Too Much Democracy or Too Little?" Unpublished manuscript.

Hirschman, A. O. 1970. *Exit, Voice and Loyalty: Responses to Decline in Firms, Organizations and States*. Cambridge: Harvard University Press.

Hodgkinson, Harold. 1991, September. "Reform Versus Reality." *Phi Delta Kappan*, 9–16.

Hogan, David. 1991. "Parent Choice, Rational Choice and the Social Constitution of Choice." Unpublished manuscript.

Jencks, Christopher. 1985. "How Much Do High School Students Learn?" *Sociology of Education* 58: 128–35.

Jencks, Christopher, et al. 1972. *Inequality*. New York: Basic Books.

Johnson, Clifford M., Andrew M. Sum, and James D. Weill. 1992. *Vanishing Dreams: The Economic Plight of America's Young Families*. Washington, D.C.: Children's Defense Fund.

Kane, Jeffrey. 1992. "Choice: The Fundamentals Revisited." In Peter W. Cookson, Jr., ed., *The Choice Controversy* (pp. 46–64). Newbury Park, Calif.: Corwin.

Kennedy, Paul M. 1989. *The Rise and Fall of the Great Powers: Economic Change and Military Conflict from 1500 to 2000*. New York: Vintage.

Kozol, Jonathan. 1991. *Savage Inequalities: Children in America's Schools*. New York: Crown.

————. 1992. Unpublished manuscript.

Lasch, Christopher. 1979. *The Culture of Narcissism*. New York: W. W. Norton.

Lee, Valerie E. 1993. "Educational Choice: The Stratifying Effects of Selecting Schools and Courses." *Educational Policy* 7:125–48.

Lee, Valerie E., and Anthony S. Bryk. 1989. "A Multilevel Model of the Social Distribution of High School Achievement." *Sociology of Education* 62: 172–92.

Lieberman, Myron. 1989. *Privatization and Educational Choice*. New York· St, Martin's.

Lukas, Anthony J. 1986. *Common Ground*. New York: Vintage.

MacLeod, Jay. 1987. *Ain't No Making It: Leveled Aspirations in a Low-Income Neighborhood*. Boulder, Colo.: Westview.

Meier, Deborah. 1987, Fall. "Success in East Harlem." *American Educator*, 34–39.

Metz, Mary Heywood. 1986. *Different by Design*. New York: Routledge.

Meyer, John. 1972. "The Effects of the Institutionalization of College in Society." In K. A. Feldman, ed., *Selected Readings in the Social Psychology of Higher Education* (pp. 109–26). New York: Pergamon.

Moore, D. R., and S. Davenport. 1990. "School Choice: The New Improved Sorting Machine." In W. L. Boyd and H. J. Walberg, eds., *Choice in Education: Potentials and Problems*. Berkeley, Calif.: McCutchan.

Nasar, Sylvia. 1992, March 5. "The 1980s: A Very Good Time for the Very Rich." *New York Times*, A1, D14.

Nathan, Joe. 1991. *Free to Teach: Achieving Equity and Excellence in Schools*. New York: Pilgrim.

Nathan, Joe, and Wayne Jennings. 1990. "Access to Opportunity: Experience of the Minnesota Students in Four Statewide School Choice Programs, 1989–90." Minneapolis: Center for School Change, University of Minnesota.

National Commission on Excellence in Education. 1983. *A Nation at Risk: The Imperative for Educational Reform*. Washington, D.C.: U.S. Government Printing Office.

National Elementary School Center. 1992. "Responding to the Needs of Today's Children." Unpublished manuscript.

National Governors' Association. 1986. *A Time for Results*. Washington, D.C.: The Association.

Office of Educational Research and Improvement. 1992. *Getting Started: How Choice Can Renew Your Public Schools*. Washington, D.C.: U.S. Government Printing Office.

Olson, Lynn. 1990, Sept. 12. "Choice Plan's Architect Relishes Her Role as State Legislature's 'Lone Independent.'" *Education Week*, 14–15.

———. 1992, Nov. 4. "Advocates React Angrily to Study Questioning Merits of Choice." *Education Week*, 5.

Olson, Mancur, Jr. 1965. *The Logic of Collective Action: Public Goods and the Theory of Groups*. Cambridge: Harvard University Press.

Paulu, Nancy. 1989. *Improving Schools and Empowering Parents: Choice in American Education*. Washington, D.C.: U.S. Government Printing Office.

Perpich, Rudy. 1989, March 6. "Choose Your School." *New York Times*, A17.

Persell, Caroline Hodges, and Peter W. Cookson, Jr. 1982. *The Effective Principal in Action*. Reston, Va.: National Association of Secondary School Principals.

———. 1985. "Chartering and Bartering: Elite Education and Social Reproduction." *Social Problems* 33(2): 114–29.

———. 1992. *Making Sense of Society.* New York: HarperCollins.

Persell, Caroline Hodges, Sophia Catsambis, and Peter W. Cookson, Jr. 1992a. "Differential Asset Conversion: Class and Gendered Pathways to Selective Colleges." *Sociology of Education* 65(3): 208–25.

———. 1992b. "Family Background, School Type, and College Attendance: A Conjoint System of Cultural Capital Transmission." *Journal of Research on Adolescence* 2(1): 1–23.

Phillips, Kevin. 1990. *The Politics of Rich and Poor.* New York: Random House.

Plank, Stephen, Kathryn Schiller, Barbara Schneider, and James S. Coleman. 1992. "Choice in Education: Some Effects." Paper delivered at "Choice: What Role in American Education?" Sponsored by the Economic Policy Institute, Washington, D.C.

Popkewitz, Thomas S. 1988. "Educational Reform: Rhetoric, Ritual and Social Interests." *Educational Theory* 38: 77–93.

———. 1991. *A Political Sociology of Educational Reform.* New York: Teachers College Press.

Powell, Arthur G., Eleanor Farrar, and David K. Cohen. 1985. *The Shopping Mall High School.* Boston: Houghton Mifflin.

Ravitch, Diane. 1974. *The Great School Wars.* New York: Basic Books.

Raywid, Mary A. 1987. "Public Choice, Yes; Vouchers, No!" *Phi Delta Kappan* 68(10): 762–69.

Riesman, David, with Nathan Glazer and Reuel Denney. 1950. *The Lonely Crowd: A Study of the Changing American Character.* New Haven: Yale University Press.

Sciulli, David. 1991. "Four Weaknesses in Rational Choice Theory's Contribution to Comparative Research." Paper presented at the American Sociological Association, Cincinnati.

Simon, Herbert. 1987. "Rationality in Psychology and Economics." In Robin M. Hogarth and Melvin W. Reder, eds., *Rational Choice: The Contrast between Economics and Psychology* (pp. 25–40). Chicago: University of Chicago Press.

Sizer, Theodore R. 1984. *Horace's Compromise: The Dilemma of the American High School*. Boston: Houghton Mifflin.

Thernstrom, Abigail. 1991, May 13. "Out-Classed." *New Republic*, 12–14.

Toch, Thomas. 1991, July 15. "The Wizard of Education." *U.S. News and World Report*, 46.

Trombley, William. 1992, Jan. 22. "Educators Group Calls School Voucher Ballot Proposal 'Evil.'" *Los Angeles Times*, A3.

Twentieth Century Fund, Task Force on Elementary and Secondary Education Policy. 1983. *Making the Grade*. New York: The Fund.

Tyack, David B. 1974. *The One Best System: A History of American Urban Education*. Cambridge: Harvard University Press.

United States Department of Education. 1991, April 18. *America 2000: An Education Strategy*. Washington, D.C.: U.S. Government Printing Office.

———. 1992, April 24. *Parental Choice in Education*. Washington, D.C.: Office of Intergovernmental and Interagency Affairs.

Waldman, Steven. 1992, Jan. 27. "The Tyranny of Choice." *New Republic*, 22–25.

Walford, Geoffrey. 1992. "Educational Choice and Equity in Great Britain." *Educational Policy* 6(2): 123–38.

Walsh, Mark. 1992, Jan. 29. "Private-School, Religious Groups Join to Back President's Choice Proposal." *Education Week*, 23.

Wells, Amy Stuart. 1991. "The Sociology of School Choice: A Study of Black Students' Participation in a Voluntary Transfer Plan." Ph.D. diss., Teachers College, Columbia University.

White, Merry. 1987. *The Japanese Educational Challenge*. New York: Free Press.

Wilkerson, Isabel. 1992, Dec. 16. "Des Moines Acts to Halt White Flight after State Allows Choice of Schools." *New York Times*, B9.

Willms, J. Douglas, and Frank H. Echols. 1992. "The Scottish Experience of Parental Choice of Schools." Paper presented at "Choice: What Role in American Education?" Sponsored by the Economic Policy Institute, Washington, D.C.

Witte, John F. 1990. "Choice and Control in American Education: An Analytical Overview." In William H. Clune and John F. Witte, eds., *Choice and Control in American Education*. Vol. 1: *The Theory of Choice and Control in Education* (pp. 11–46). New York: Falmer.

———. 1992. "The Milwaukee Private-School Parental Choice Program." Paper delivered at "Choice: What Role in American Education?" Sponsored by the Economic Policy Institute, Washington, D.C.

Zweigenhaft, Richard L., and G. William Domhoff. 1991. *Blacks in the White Establishment? A Study of Race and Class in America*. New Haven: Yale University Press.

Index

Bilingual education, 76
Black power movement, 28
Blackman, J., 75
Blacks. *See* African-Americans
Blank, Rolf K., 76
Blodgett, Bonnie, 49–50
Bolick, Clint, 30
Boston, Mass., 29
Bourdieu, Pierre, 95
Bowles, Samuel, 23
Boyer, Ernest L., 72
Bridge, R. G., 75
Brown, Frank, 114–15
Brown v. Board of Education, 27
Bryk, Anthony S., 81
Burrow, Bill, 68
Bush, George, 7, 16, 34, 36, 43, 57, 65, 68
Business Higher Education Forum, 18
Busing, 29, 66, 77

Cain, G. G., 80
California: voucher proposal in, 6, 39, 75–76, 141; racial mix of schools in, 12, 25; choice legislation in, 39, 40, 140–41; Alum Rock School District, 75–76, 91; Richmond Unified School District, 104, 140
Calvin, John, 105
Cambridge, Mass., 58–60, 90
Canada, 113, 115
Capell, F., Jr., 75, 78
Capitalism, 103–07. *See also* Market metaphors
Carnegie Forum on Education and the Economy, 19
Carnegie Foundation, 71–72, 86
Carnegie Foundation for the

Advancement of Teaching, 8, 18
Catholic Daughters of America, 31
Catholic Golden Age, 31
Catholic schools, 32, 80, 81, 91–92, 105. *See also* Private schools
Catsambis, Sophia, 96
Cavazos, Lauro F., 113
Center for Choice in Education, 30, 42
Chambers, Raymond, 33
Charter schools, 15, 40, 41, 44, 46, 141, 145, 150
Chavez, Linda, 33
Chicago Reform Act, 19
Child-benefit theory, 128–30
Children and children's rights, 3, 12–14, 122–23, 126, 127
Children's Defense Fund, 13
Christian Schools International, 31
Chubb, John E., 25, 33, 36, 83–86
Civil libertarians, 21–23, 30
Clinchy, Evans, 30
Clinton, Bill, 42
Clune, William H., 73–74
Coalition of Essential Schools, 52
Cohen, David K., 25
Coleman, James S., 33, 80–83, 86, 92, 94, 107
College Board, 18
Colorado, 39, 141
Community, 10, 97–98
Connecticut, 40, 141
Consumerism. *See* Market metaphors
Controlled choice, 14, 15, 56–64, 69, 94, 130
Cookson, Peter W., Jr., 12, 22, 55, 72, 76–77, 79, 82, 88, 89, 95–96, 110, 112, 126
Coombs, Philip H., 112

France, 26, 113, 116
Friedman, Milton, 28, 29
Friends Council on Education, 31
Fundamentalists. *See* Protestant
    fundamentalists

G.I. Bill Opportunity Scholarships for
    Children, 7, 65
"Garbage-can theory of organizational
    decision-making," 8–9
Georgia, 142
Germany, 26, 113
Gibbs, Nancy, 3
Gilder, Richard, Jr., 33
Gintis, Herbert, 23
Glazer, Nathan, 33, 101
Glenn, Charles L., 30, 56–58, 113–14
Glenn, Colman, 33
Goldberger, A. S., 80
Golden Rule Insurance Co., 41, 42
Goldwater, Barry, 102, 103
Goodlad, John, 18
Great Britain, 92, 113, 116–18
Grover, Herbert J., 67
Guffanti, Stephen, 6

Harrington, Diane, 55, 77, 89
Harrington, Michael, 28
Hartmann, David, 68
Hawaii, 25, 142
Hawthorne effect, 55
Health care, 82–83
Heritage Foundation, 30, 31
Hess, G. Alfred, Jr., 19
Hickel, Walter, 139
Hispanics, 51–52, 63, 66, 76, 92
Hodgkinson, Harold, 3
Hoffer, Thomas, 80–83

Hogan, David, 109–10
Homo economicus, 101–05
Houle, Fred, 62
Idaho, 142
Illinois, 19, 42, 142–43
Immigrants and immigration, 2, 12, 37,
    50, 61, 92
Income. *See* Poverty; Wealth
Indiana, 42, 143
Indianapolis, Ind., 42
Individualism, 5, 9, 10, 102–06, 123
Inner-city schools. *See* Private schools;
    Public schools
"Inner-directed man," 101
"Inner-directed" school reform, 121–23
Institute for Independent Education, 31
Institute for Responsive Education, 30
Integration, 27–29, 68, 95, 130
Interdistrict choice, 15, 39, 94, 130
Intersectional choice, 15
Intradistrict choice, 14
Intrasectional choice, 15
Iowa, 25, 39, 143
Israel, 113, 116

Jackson, Jesse, 65
Japan, 12, 24, 26, 106
Jencks, Christopher, 64, 75, 81, 112
Jennings, Wayne, 45
Jesuit Secondary Education
    Association, 31
Johnson, Clifford M., 13
Johnson, Lyndon, 28
Kamia, Dick, 41
Kane, Jeffrey, 21–22
Kansas, 40–41, 143
Kean, Thomas, 33
Kennedy, Paul, 11

168

inorities: in public schools, 4, 25; and racism, 12; poverty of, 13; de facto segregation of, 27–28; and busing, 29, 77; and legislated equity, 31; in New York City, 4, 51–52; in White Plains, N.Y., 63; in Milwaukee, 66, 97; responses to school choice by, 92–94, 109. *See also* African-Americans; Hispanics

Mississippi, 25, 145

Missouri, 109, 146

Mitterand, François, 116

Model schools, 131, 133–34

Moe, Terry M., 25, 36, 72, 83–86

Montana, 146

Moore, D. R., 90

Mueller v. Allen, 43

Nasar, Sylvia, 13

Nathan, Joe, 30, 33, 42–43, 45, 72, 89, 124

Nation at Risk, A, 18

Nation Prepared, A, 19

National Association of Episcopal Schools, 31

National Association of Independent Schools, 31

National Association of Private Schools for Exceptional Children, 31

National Catholic Educational Association, 31

National Center for Neighborhood Enterprise, 42

National Coalition for the Improvement and Reform of American Education, 31

National Commission on Excellence in Education, 18

National Council on Catholic Women, 31

National Elementary School Center, 122–23

National Governors Association, 18

National Governors' Conference *(1986)*, 34

National School Choice Demonstration Projects, 36

National Society of Hebrew Day Schools, 31

Nebraska, 39, 146

Netherlands, 114–15

Nevada, 146

New American Schools Development Corporation, 16

New Hampshire, 25, 146–47

New Jersey, 41, 147

New Mexico, 25, 147

New Paradigm, 34, 103–04

New York City: statistics on public schools in, 25; East Harlem Community School District 4, 50–55, 69, 77–79, 89, 124, 125, 147; structure of public school system in, 50–51; magnet schools in, 93; Community School District *1*, 124–25; Community School District *2*, 125

New York state: school-based management in, 19; White Plains schools, 62–64, 90; choice legislation in, 147–48. *See also* New York City

North Carolina, 148

North Dakota, 148

Ohio, 39, 148

Oklahoma, 148

Olson, Lynn, 65, 66

Olson, Mancur, Jr., 106
Open enrollment, 14, 41, 147
Oregon, 22, 39, 42, 149
"Outer-directed man," 101
"Outer-directed" school reform, 101, 121

PACE (Parents Advocating Choice in Education), 42
Paine, Thomas, 21
Pallas, Aaron, 80, 81
Parent information centers, 59–64, 90, 98, 136
Parents for Educational Choice, 6
Passeron, Jean-Claude, 95
Patterson, Senator, 40
Paulu, Nancy, 34, 35, 77–78
Pennsylvania, 33, 39, 42, 149
Perpich, Rudy, 23–24, 43–44
Persell, Caroline Hodges, 12, 76–77, 79, 82, 88, 95–96, 110, 126
Peterkin, Robert S., 33, 68
Phillips, Kevin, 13
Phyllis Schlafly Report, 30
Pierce v. The Society of Sisters, 22
Plank, Stephen, 86, 94
Plessy v. Ferguson, 27
Poland, 113, 116
Polanyi, Karl, 100
Popkewitz, Thomas S., 9
Postsecondary options, 15
Poverty, 3, 12–14, 28, 51–55, 66–67
Powell, Arthur G., 25
Price, Perry, 48, 49
Principals, 76–77
Private schools: as alternative, 1; and fundamentalists, 4; franchising of, 16; court cases on, 22; funding of,

22–23, 32, 129; statistics on, 24, 32; and school choice, 31–32; mythology of, 69–70; and parents, 69; student achievement in, 80–83; income of families in, 82; and equity, 95–97; and social status, 95–96, 111; in inner city, 128–29. See also Catholic schools
Protestant fundamentalists, 4, 29–30, 65, 105
Public schools: crisis in, 2–4, 27; inner-city schools, 2–3, 28, 50–55, 119; minorities in, 4, 25; and class structure, 23; decentralized and diverse system of, 23–27; statistics on, 24–25; curriculum and pedagogy in, 25–26, 29; integration of 27–29, 68; segregation of, 27, 39, 95; student achievement in, compared with private schools, 80–83; improvement of, and school choice, 87–90. See also Education; School choice; and specific locations

Rand Corporation, 75–76
Rational-choice theory, 107–12
Ravitch, Diane, 21, 30
Raywid, Mary Anne, 30, 33, 89, 124
REACH (Road to Educational Achievement through Choice), 33, 42
Reagan, Ronald, 6–7, 17–18, 29, 57, 65, 101–03
Reform. See School reform
Republican party, 30, 34, 39, 68
Research, 72–87
Rhode Island, 149
Richmond, Calif., 104, 140
Riesman, David, 101

Robertson, Pat, 7
Rochester, N.Y., 19
Rooney, Pat, 41, 42
Roosevelt, Franklin D., 9

Sadovnik, Alan R., 112
St. Louis, 109
St. Paul, Minn., 47–49
Sartre, Jean-Paul, 11
Schiller, Kathryn, 86, 92, 94
Schlesinger, Arthur, Jr., 12
Schneider, Barbara, 86, 92, 94
School choice: cultural context of, 1–16; as movement, 4–8, 29–36; and market metaphors, 5, 36, 83–87, 99–120; proponents of, 6–8, 29–36, 39; and commodification, 8–14; "garbage-can theory of organizational decision-making," 8–9; "state-relative-autonomy" theory of, 8; and lifestyle loyalties, 10–11; and doubt about future direction of society, 11–12; and polarization by wealth and income, 12–14; definitions of, 14–16; political roots and philosophical origins of, 17–37; origins of, 20–23; and civil libertarians, 21–23, 30; proximate causes of, 27–29; and "white flight," 27, 115; new-right conservatives' support for, 29–36; and lobbying establishment, 31–33; opponents of, 33; benefits of, 35; market rationale for, 36; state legislation on, 38–42, 139–52; case studies on, 42–68; in Minnesota, 42–50, 55, 89, 145; in New York City, 50–55, 77–79, 89, 124–25, 147; Massachusetts model of, 55–64,

90, 144–45; in White Plains, N.Y., 62–64, 90; in Wisconsin, 64–68, 82, 96–97, 152; complexity of, 69–70; assessment of outcomes, 71–98; research on, 74–77; and student achievement, 77–87, 98; and school improvement, 87–90, 98; and equity, 90–98; and educated parents, 91–94; and community, 97–98; and social trust, 98; as "outer-directed" school reform, 101, 121; in California, 104, 140–41; and capitalism, 106–07; rational-choice theory applied to, 110–12; international perspectives on, 112–18; proposal for managed school choice, 130, 133–34. *See also* School reform
School reform: "inner-directed," 121–23; and authenticity, 123–27; and active knowledge, 126–27; and attachment, 126; and equality, 127–31; new educational convenant, 127–31; and self-reliance, 127; and funding, 130, 132–33; managed school choice, 130, 133–34; educational trust fund, 131–33, 135–36; model schools, 131, 133–34; proposal for, 131–34; implementation issues for, 134; distribution of educational shares, 135–36; and consumer protection, 136–37; parent information centers, 136. *See also* School choice
Sciulli, David, 108
Scotland, 109, 116–17
Second-chance programs, 15
Segregation, 27–28, 39, 95